On Being Raped

On Being Raped

Raymond M. Douglas

Beacon Press
Boston

Beacon Press
Boston, Massachusetts
www.beacon.org

Beacon Press books
are published under the auspices of
the Unitarian Universalist Association of Congregations.

19 18 17 16   8 7 6 5 4 3 2 1

This book is printed on acid-free paper that meets the uncoated paper
ANSI/NISO specifications for permanence as revised in 1992.

Text design and composition by Kim Arney

Library of Congress Cataloging-in-Publication Data

Names: Douglas, R. M.
Title: On being raped / Raymond M. Douglas.
Description: Boston : Beacon Press, [2016]
Identifiers: LCCN 2015030708 |
    ISBN 9780807050941 (hardcover : alk. paper) |
    ISBN 9780807050958 (ebook)
Subjects: LCSH: Douglas, R. M. | Male rape victims. |
    Male rape. | Male rape—Psychological aspects.
Classification: LCC HV6558 .D68 2016 | DDC 362.8830811—dc23
    LC record available at http://lccn.loc.gov/2015030708

For all the others

Contents

1

On Being Raped

IT'S NOT EVIL THAT'S BANAL, IT'S EVILDOERS. GREAT CRIMES have a grandeur to them, a dramatic sweep that compels our attention. Even petty offenses can be interesting, like the wave of kidnappings of lawn ornaments for ransom in the northeastern United States a few years ago. But the perpetrators of even the most atrocious deeds seem to have nothing in common beyond their personal insignificance. Adolf Hitler was an awkward nonentity, his stock of knowledge drawn from the early twentieth-century Viennese equivalent of the *Reader's Digest*, with herbicidal bad breath and an over-large nose to divert attention from which he grew a still more ridiculous moustache. Joseph Stalin was a failed priest. Bonnie and Clyde were, respectively, a part-time waitress and an unsuccessful turkey thief. Hermann Goering played with trains. Hence the frustration of biographers who peel away layer after layer of the psyches of history's greatest criminals only to discover, in Gertrude Stein's words, that there is no there there.

The man who raped me conforms all too faithfully to this pattern. I knew little about him before the attack, and have not seen any reason to find out much more since then. Undistinguished in his career, unexceptional in appearance and demeanor, there was nothing about him that would make him stand out in a crowd. It was my bad luck to learn that he was also cunning, violent, and someone who obtained gratification from causing others to suffer. But even those traits are not particularly unusual in today's world. Not the least embarrassing aspect of this entire episode is that my life should have been so deeply affected in so many ways by so entirely mundane an individual.

As for the rape itself, it too, as best as I can judge, was mundane. To be sure, that's largely guesswork on my part. There is only one rape that I can claim to know about with any degree of authority, and that is my own. And yet even as I write about it, I can see the words fade and lose definition before my eyes. How many billions of times have such things happened in human history? How many tens of thousands of descriptions? Everything lapses into a terrible sameness, a story that isn't worth telling because it is so infuriatingly familiar. What makes my rape different? "Well, it happened to *me*" hardly seems like a compelling justification for banging on about it. No bore like a rape bore.

But there's the difficulty. My rape, in all important respects like everybody else's, fits every pattern but my own. Since it happened, I've been trying to find a slot for it in my biography, with clearly marked boundaries like all the other highlights (birth, school years, first job, rape, university, grad school . . .). But it refuses to stay there. Even today it's continuing to rewrite the computer code of my life, like one of those pieces of Web malware that covers the screen with pop-up windows faster than I can close them down. I've experienced other crimes, as most people have: burglary, property theft, minor assaults. There one can speak of a "before" and "after." The baddie was identified and prosecuted, or not; the goods were recovered or the insurance policy paid off; the drunken creep who started swinging wildly in all directions was thrown out by the bouncer. Only in this instance are things different. Through the intervention of some inexplicable chronological constant, rape is always now.

I suspect that this is true for others also, though since being raped I've become much more cautious about telling anybody else what their experience is like. The really difficult thing is to say why I have found it so. There have been many events in my life that I, at any rate, found momentous: some good, some gruesome. Why can't this single night, out of all of them, be relegated to the place it belongs—an unpleasant experience from my past, but one that was survived and surmounted?

The answer, I think, is that rape—my rape, anyway; probably most other people's also—doesn't allow for that kind of separation between the event and the self. Rape is knowledge, but not the sort that does you, or anybody else, any good. When I was raped, I learned things about myself and the world I live in that it would have been far better never to know. And for most of my adult life, the knowledge has been killing me.

.   .   .

I was eighteen years of age. My second job out of school was as the lone security guard on the night shift at a teacher-training college: six days on, Fridays off. I patrolled the seven-acre campus with a flashlight and a dog that did its damnedest to bite me every time I put the leash on until I finally insisted that the canine lunatic be taken away. The hours were long and the pay abysmal, but I liked the work and the responsibility.

One rainy February evening on my off night, a priest of my acquaintance telephoned my home and left a message with my mother asking me to come down to the parochial house, where he was having a gathering. I knew him to talk to, though this was the first such invitation I'd received and I hadn't laid eyes on him in months. He'd been a kind of unofficial chaplain at my school, much involved in conducting spiritual retreats, and a lot of the older students used to go across the street and hang out in his upstairs living room during my last year there. His music collection was locally famous, and would have been sufficient to meet the needs of a small radio station. He was in his early forties, mordant, cynical, and quick-witted. We all thought he drank a bit too much. He made clear that we were welcome to share the stock of his impressive home bar to our hearts' content, though surprisingly few of us used to take him up on the offer.

The party, when I arrived a little after nine, was something of a downer. Another priest and half a dozen or so of my erstwhile school friends were already there, three of them sitting by the fireside in the living room with grimly polite expressions on their faces. I found the remainder skulking in the adjacent kitchen, where they evidently intended to remain as long as they decently could. Our clerical host's mood, we knew, tended to ebb and flow with his alcohol consumption. When I arrived he was visibly hammered, standing at the fireside and waving a tumbler of neat whiskey around while delivering his favorite harangue of a conventionally anti-Vatican variety. We'd heard it all before, many times. As the evening dragged on, his gestures became wilder, his eyes glassier, and his rate of intake more rapid. One of my more astute friends, recognizing the danger signs, volunteered to mix the drinks. By midnight the priest seemed not to realize, or to care, that the glasses we were handing him contained little more than amber-tinged water.

Around two in the morning, the other cleric having long since fled and with no end in sight, most of us ducked into the kitchen for a quick council of war. We agreed that our man was in no condition to be left on his own; apart from anything else, his car stood outside the house, as it always did in readiness for a late call-out to some dying parishioner's bedside, and none of us knew where he kept the keys. Clearly he had no intention of winding down operations as long as the party was under way. Straws were drawn, and it fell to me to stay with him after the others departed; ensure that he did not go on any midnight drives by himself; and pour him into bed whenever the impact of the booze he had already consumed finally knocked him over.

More than an hour later, the fire having gone out and a chill having descended on the room, the priest finally agreed to my diplomatic suggestions that it was time for us both to grab forty winks. His bedroom lay directly off the living room, via a pair of sliding wooden doors. He rummaged around the wardrobe, pulling out a couple of blankets and a pillow and coming back to toss them on the sofa for me while I raked out the last embers from the grate. I was a little surprised when he crossed over and locked from the inside the door of the apartment leading to the hallway. "Oh, I always do that," he said, "we've had several break-ins over the years." I didn't think much of it at the time.

Manual dexterity problems delayed the process of retiring for the night. After watching my host sitting on the side of his bed fumbling ineffectually at his laces for several minutes, I knelt at his feet, removed his shoes, and helped him laboriously undress and struggle into his pajamas and his bed. This done, I turned to leave. "No, wait a minute," he called in alarm. "I can't get to sleep on my own in the dark. Stay with me until I drop off. I've had a skinful. It won't take long. Please?"

Anything for a quiet life. I drew up a chair. "No, don't be ridiculous," he said crossly. "You can lie down on the bed. There's any amount of room. I'll be out like a light in ten minutes. Just kick your shoes off. I don't want you messing up my quilt." Without waiting for a reply, he reached across and flicked out the bedside light.

At this point, you're doubtless drawing the conclusion that if I fell for that one, I deserved anything I got. And now we have the first invariable component of the rape script: the list of charges. Prisoner at the bar, how could you have been so stupid? What did you think he was going to do? Don't you realize that you were asking for it? Do you really expect the members of the jury to believe that you didn't know what was coming next?

In fact I didn't. The thought never so much as crossed my mind. He was a priest. I was a parishioner, and a former pupil. I was also a virgin, although that was hardly relevant because the notion that anything sexual might occur in my current surroundings was as remote to me as the idea of an asteroid's materializing that night to demolish the Earth.

The long curtains were very effective. Not a chink of light reached the bedroom from the dim illuminations outside the window. In the pitch-blackness I groped my way to the edge of the bed and stretched out gingerly on the left-hand side. He was right; there was plenty of room. Lying on my back, I listened for the sound of his breathing, hoping that it would soon become slow and regular enough to allow me to crawl away quietly to the sofa that awaited me. It had been a very long day, and I too badly wanted my sleep. If I wasn't careful, it would be all too easy to doze off where I was.

Perhaps ten minutes passed. Then a hand emerged from the darkness and attached itself to my waistband. The other followed, working at my belt buckle. Startled, I began to sit up. The first hand disengaged, placed itself on my breastbone and pressed me firmly down again. A voice spoke in low but emphatic tones from what seemed to be a range of inches into my right ear—an authoritative voice, brooking no argument.

"I want you to suck me."

Ours was an unsophisticated culture at the time. Americanisms like "blow job" had not yet entered the vernacular. For a comical second or two—had anybody had a pair of infrared goggles, my expression must have been priceless—I tried to fathom what this cryptic request might mean. Renewed vigorous jerks at my trousers, though, caused the penny to drop fairly quickly. Again the voice, this time louder and more menacing. "Suck me."

Not good. Time to be elsewhere. I rolled toward the edge of the bed, a sensible idea that occurred to me a second too late. The weight of a body landed squarely on top of me, not gently. For the first time I had reason to notice that the priest was very much heavier than I was and seemed a good deal more powerful into the bargain. I lunged upward. A heavy forearm came down like a bar across my throat, pinning me to the surface of the bed by my neck. It hurt like blazes, and I would have produced a yell of pain and surprise if it had not also cut off my breathing. With his other hand, the priest reached across and turned on the bedside light. Now he leaned back, releasing my neck and straddling my hips, with his knees near my shoulders, staring down at me as if awaiting my next move.

I don't believe that either of us said anything for several moments after that. I know I didn't. The situation seemed quite clear, with further discussion unnecessary. What was less obvious was what I should do next. Ludicrously, resorting to a tactic that seemed more appropriate to the school playground than the situation in which I found myself, I tried to heave him off me. When you are lying on your back with someone sitting on top of you, the only movement of which you are capable is a series of rapid upward pelvic thrusts, a grotesque parody of the motions of sexual intercourse. The irony was lost upon me at the time. Anyway it didn't work. My captor held his position with ease while I thrashed and flailed beneath him, waiting for me to stop. He didn't seem nearly as alcoholically impaired as he had been twenty minutes previously.

My arms were still free, so I fought. It wasn't any kind of conscious decision, no weighing of tactics or options. Had I had time to consider my position, I might have concluded that in this situation, compliance was the better part of valor. But the impulse to ball my fists and start doing some real damage seemed to me as natural as breathing. Nor was I expecting to fail.

There is a conviction that all males over the age of twelve, or nearly all, share: when the chips are truly down, if you are fighting for your life, you will find within you the strength to prevail over anyone who isn't fighting for his. I don't think that this is the result of the influence of Hollywood films, or at any rate not of those alone. It's the nearest thing I know of to a core constituent of maleness, our psychic ace in the hole. It allows us to go through dangerous parts of town without worrying, or even thinking, too much about it. It makes us believe that if we have to fight in wars we may perhaps die, but we certainly won't be the first ones to be killed. The reason films like *Die Hard* resonate among men may in fact be that they appeal to this sense already preprogrammed within us, that those reserves are there to be called upon when we need them, and that they will not then fail us.

So I lashed out, as violently as I could, with every ounce of adrenalin-fuelled desperation that I possessed. I was trying to hurt, putting all the strength I could muster

into my blows from my less-than-favorable prone position, looking for vulnerable spots, throwing elbows as
well as fists. I would probably have sunk my teeth into
him if I had been able to reach him that way. I had never
behaved in a more primitive manner in my life, leaving
nothing I could think of untried, grunting with effort like
a Wimbledon tennis player with each punch, scrabbling
for sensitive places where I might gouge, squeeze, or twist.

It wasn't nearly enough, not by the longest shot. And
I can truthfully say that the making of that discovery produced greater consternation in me than anything that had
occurred in my life to that point. I had connected with a
few punches, to be sure, but the priest absorbed them with
relative ease and deflected the rest. Now he responded.
The first riposte (fist? elbow? implement? I still have no
idea) came out of nowhere, catching me on the right side
of the skull, above the ear, with unimaginable force, jerk-
ing my head to the edge of the bed and causing me to
bite my tongue, it seemed, almost in two. A second was
not necessary. My peripheral vision disappeared, so that I
could see only a narrow field filled almost entirely by his
face directly above me. A wave of nausea, accompanied
by electric shocks of pain that were synchronized with my
pulse, monopolized my consciousness. To my shame, that
single devastating blow was all it took to subdue me. I
could not absorb another. The fight drained out of me like

a discharged electrical battery, and I lay completely still. This, it seemed, was what the priest had been waiting for. He raised himself up from across my thighs; slammed a sharp knee into the pit of my stomach, driving what little breath I still had out of me; wriggled out of his pajama bottoms; and started.

2

On Inconvenient Truths

———— •• ————

HUMAN LIFE HAS A TIRESOME WAY OF NOT FITTING IN WITH established categories. This is another reason why I am reluctant to generalize from my particular experience. Nowadays when a rainy night in late February obtrudes itself into my consciousness, the words that attach themselves to those hours are a dyad, "rape-torture." The two for me have become inseparable, to the point that I can't truly say I know what "rape" is like at all.

For years that was a term from which I fled. It didn't describe me. Of course nothing I could think of did, but not *that* word especially. In my ongoing internal monologue, I would admit to myself that I had experienced an "attack." That was surely incontrovertible. Sometimes

I might permit my inner voice to speak of "sexual assault"—not often, and with heavy qualifications. (What kind of sexual assault, prisoner at the bar? Be specific, please. Sodomy? Molestation? Forcible carnal knowledge? Defilement of a virgin?)

That was as far as I could go. The "r" word terrified me for all sorts of reasons: its monosyllabic ugliness, its brutal specificity, above all its connection to so many other words that described a universe of suffering that was at once fundamentally bound up with and completely different from my own. To use it meant to start learning a foreign language, a difficult one like Arabic or Japanese that would never accurately describe what I wanted to say. The characters, the metaphors, of that foreign tongue had all been designed for another purpose. One learns a language to communicate, to express and to understand; this one would forever circumscribe and distort the reality of my experience, cutting off some aspects and stretching others into grotesque, disturbing shapes.

Still, it came close enough to the truth to be unbearable. The sight of the "r" word was enough to produce reactions in me that ran the gamut from the unsettling to the disastrous. I became skilled at avoidance, policing my reading of newspapers and books with a diligence and rigor that would have deeply gratified the Christian Brothers who had once taught my thirteen-year-old classmates and myself about the paramount importance of maintaining "custody of the eyes." But though it was easier to avoid such things in a considerably less rape-saturated culture than the one we have now, failures occurred nonetheless. Nor was the danger to be found in visual materials alone, but in all manner of things—a whiff of aftershave, the clap of an acquaintance's hand on my shoulder—that could catch me by surprise with some unexpected association. Once I shattered a cheap portable radio into a thousand pieces on the kitchen floor when I wasn't able to turn off "Moments in Love" by the Art of Noise quickly enough.

In the past couple of years I've stopped running away from the term. It hadn't lost its power to cause me discomfort, which immediately made me question whether I was now embracing it because I *wanted* to be upset by it. (One of the wondrous aspects of rape is how it trains you to come up with the most discreditable explanation possible for whatever you happen to be doing at any given time.) I didn't suppose that doing so would diminish that feeling through some process of desensitization, and so far I've been right about that. But the fact remained that every other description I'd come up with was a lie, and not even a vaguely plausible one. Like most liars, I was finding it too difficult to keep my story straight, even though I was the only one who had to be taken in by it.

Not everybody agrees with my choice of words, though the law in the country of my birth has moved along with me in that direction. Legally, at any rate, my attack now "counts," and my rapist could be prosecuted under that heading, though somehow I doubt the knowledge keeps him awake at night. In the place in which I live today, he could not. The statute in my current state of residence reserves that term for the forcible insertion of a penis into a vagina—a definition that allows me, other similarly situated men, and innumerable women whose attacks did not conform to that particular model, to experience the perverse charm of switching between the ranks of the raped and the unraped merely by stepping on board an airplane for a few hours.

That's the law. In reality, rape is not truly about what organ or object penetrated which orifice but, to borrow another legal term, the totality of the circumstances. In my case, which isn't, after all, such an interesting or exceptional one, those circumstances included the intentional infliction of pain upon me, of an intensity and a duration with which I was not previously familiar. Whether that should be considered "rape accompanied by torture," or "rape accomplished through torture," is no longer interesting to me. I can't separate the two elements, even conceptually, and I don't see the point in trying.

. . .

In that upstairs bedroom I had fought—if one can so describe a flat-on-my-back exhibition of what in the school-
yards of my youth we wryly used to describe as "handbags
at ten paces"—to avoid whatever my attacker had in mind
for me. But there are what the economists call opportunity
costs to such an action. Having first resisted, the option
of seeking to minimize the coming attack by seeming to
acquiesce was no longer available to me. Worse still, my
display of reluctance had backfired, making the priest sitting on top of me incandescently angry. His expectations
for the night's entertainment, it quickly emerged, had involved my willing, indeed enthusiastic, participation. My
initial refusal to provide it was not well received. In a way
that after reading the literature on malignant narcissism
would come to make sense to me, but at the time seemed
terrifying confirmation that I was dealing with someone
who was completely unhinged, he insisted at the top of
his lungs, punctuated by open-handed slaps across my
face, that I had been signaling my sexual receptivity to
him in many and unmistakable ways, not only that evening, but all the way back to my secondary-school days.
My croaked protestations, through a half-constricted
and painfully swollen airway, that these were never my

intentions, indeed that we hardly knew each other, had precisely the opposite effect from the one for which I was aiming. With every denial, each insistence that his perceptions and not mine were mistaken, his rage grew more ungovernable, his face contorted and his cascade of shouted words so rapid and deafening that I could hardly make them out. I owed him. Who the fuck did I think I was to be treating him like this? Did I seriously believe, after how I had behaved, that I wasn't going to be made to pay? At length, fearing that if I continued stoking the fire he would lose what little self-control remained to him and kill me on the spot, I fell silent, my tongue sticking to the roof of my mouth in dread of the ordeal that, I now recognized, I could not avoid undergoing.

Many unpleasant and squalid minutes later (Keep your expression neutral! Breathe through your nose! For the love of Mike don't throw up!), another piece of knowledge, of the profoundly-true-but-thoroughly-useless variety, was revealed to me. There are few things on this planet more dangerous than an angry rapist who is having difficulty sustaining an erection.

When one is being beaten, time speeds up in a jerky, incoherent fashion. Too much is going on too quickly for the brain to process the sequence of events, far less come up with any kind of meaningful response. While the beating was under way, I found the most oppressive element to be not the physical anguish, sickeningly intense though that was, but the mental fog that was depriving me of any ability to reason. A sense of panic overtook me. My head ricocheted from side to side, attempting to escape while the rest of my body was pinned and pounded. I emitted cries, undignified ones. Once again my visual field seemed to be affected. The experience was overwhelming and bewildering. I felt that if I could have just the shortest of respites, a few pain-free moments, I could regain control over what was happening to me. As it was, I was never able to catch up. Even my involuntary reactions—yelps, flinches, eventually full-throated howls—all seemed to be coming too late, seconds after the blows that had produced them landed. The pace, and the pain, were increasing exponentially, leaving me further and further behind, unable to draw breath.

Eventually it stopped. Don't ask me for how long it had gone on. He changed his position on the bed, sitting back with his legs parted and dragging my head toward him. We were now going to try something different. Penis, meet mouth. Hand, meet throat. Open. Squeeze. Choke. Thrust. Gag. Release. Withdraw. Open. Squeeze. Choke. Thrust. Gag. Lather, rinse, repeat.

That didn't do the trick either, though it wasn't for want of trying. Perhaps the whiskey he had consumed earlier was taking its revenge. If so, it was my enemy more than his. By now I had undergone a transformation that was marvelous to behold. At last, and far too late for it to do me any good, I was as dedicated and compliant a bedmate as my rapist's most lurid fantasies could have conjured up, as single-mindedly committed as he to the goal of coaxing some kind of sexual response out of him. But willingness is not a substitute for skill, and this was not the time for an eighteen-year-old tyro to rectify the deficiencies in his technique by on-the-job learning. The entire night, my rapist never achieved more than a state of semi-tumescence, and the orgasm for him that we sought, he with mounting frustration, I with desperation, eluded us both.

That was bad news for me, for in the rape business, payment is by results. If I couldn't discharge my debt in the conventional manner, some other form of settling the score would be required. Thus it was that he turned his attention from his own body to mine, and its vulnerabilities, in the same way that a vicious child squeezes a kitten to hear its high-pitched yowls. I call it "torture" for want of a more accurate term, although I know that between the trivial discomforts I experienced that night and true torture lies the difference between the shadow and the substance. The priest was hurting me in a state of frenzied, ungovernable anger, not cold, scientific rationality. No doubt he didn't really know how to inflict pain most effectively. Comparatively speaking, I got away lightly, very lightly indeed. Given the embarrassingly craven manner of my response to the trials I did encounter, it is just as well.

Yet if the execution was different, the psychology was the same, as were its effects. My rapist had largely given up on achieving sexual gratification, even as I writhed and twisted helplessly beneath him. He wasn't, I believe, hurting me in the hope that it would help him get hard. He was inflicting severe physical and mental pain upon me because he wanted me to experience severe physical and mental pain. Nothing more was to be gained by it. I would not become a less clumsy fellator, or a more enthusiastic participant, as a result of this treatment. In fact, from this point onward every imaginable thing that, as a human being rather than an animal, I might do was superfluous. The range of my possible functions was narrowed down to a single one. I was there in his hands to suffer. And so I did.

.　.　.

Sometime that night, though I can't tell at what precise moment, I came to realize that I was going to be killed.

It wasn't because of anything my rapist had said. I'm practically certain, though it's possible that I missed something in the torrent of words breaking over my head, that he never uttered a single threat against me. Certainly I had made no inquiries as to his intentions. ("What are you going to do to me?" is not a sensible question to ask if you aren't able to bear the answer.) My understanding followed inescapably from the logic of the situation. At some earlier point in the proceedings it would have been safe to let me go. It was not safe now.

To know for a certainty that you are living through the final hours of your life is said to concentrate the mind wonderfully. For me it did nothing of the kind. My consciousness was not heightened; if anything, it seemed to have taken French leave. I can remember almost nothing about my surroundings and would be hard put to it to draw a sketch of that bedroom with any accuracy. (Were the walls painted a salmon color, as I seem to recall, or cream? Was the carpet red or beige? Can I be certain that there *was* a carpet?) My attention was elsewhere. Very shortly now I was going to meet my Maker, and I dreaded both the prospect and, still more, the process.

I was—am—a conventional Catholic of the "pray, pay, and obey" variety. I grew up in a country where conventional Catholicism was infused into every aspect of life. In the crowd I ran with, what little adolescent rebellion against the Church that took place was fuelled more by laziness and hormones than conviction. Serious anticlericalism was rare, and was regarded by us as showing off. So too was serious piety. We mostly did what the religious and secular authority figures in our lives expected us to do; pushed the envelope of the Ten Commandments as far as we considered reasonable and safe; took few things seriously; and postponed our existential crises to some convenient future time.

For me that time was now. I had not the slightest doubt that I was about to encounter God; I just didn't think that He was going to be pleased to see me. I couldn't say whether I was in a state of grace (how long had it been since my last confession? A very long time indeed . . .). But whatever my former chances of meeting the minimum requirement for salvation had been, I was unable to avoid the thought that the past two hours had decisively tilted the scales against me. It wasn't so much that I had been engaging in what the Catechism used to describe as "unnatural" activities. I could always plead *force majeure* on that score, and not even the severest Recording Angel could reasonably make out that I had enjoyed it. The bigger problem was that in my deeds and thoughts, if not my words, I might very well have denied Him, not three times, but dozens.

In rape, one learns truth. The truth about me was that it was possible to make me act in contradiction of myself in a manner that I would have sworn with uttermost conviction only a few hours previously could never happen regardless of the circumstances. And it hadn't even taken very much. No Gestapo, no gang of knuckle-dragging convicts, was necessary to reduce me to my wretched essence, only the unimpressive figure of a sedentary middle-class man in his forties. He happened to outweigh me by sixty or seventy pounds. That single fact made all the difference. To please him I would do, and had done, everything he required of me. It was no longer possible to believe that if he chose to escalate his demands still further, there might be some intolerably outrageous or degrading sticking point at which I would suddenly develop scruples.

The Church, it transpires, has no fewer than six patron saints of rape victims: St. Agatha, St. Agnes of Rome, St. Dymphna, St. Potamiaena, St. Solange, and St. Maria Goretti. (Why so many, one might ask? but that question surely answers itself.) All of them are female, and none of them was raped. At the time I knew nothing about the first five, but Goretti's was a very familiar name to me. Her story was heavily emphasized in the Christian Doctrine textbook used during my first year of secondary school, serving as it did as a vivid illustrative example for girls of the importance of bodily purity, and for boys of the catastrophic consequences of unrestrained male lust. An eleven-year-old Italian girl, she had been repeatedly stabbed in 1902 by a farmhand neighbor, eight years her senior, while fighting off his attempt to rape her. Before dying two weeks later, she forgave her attacker. On the centenary of her martyrdom, Pope John Paul II under-lined the essential element of her story: "She did not break God's commandment in spite of being threatened by death." How had I kept God's commandment? I knew the answer. When the testing time came, I had placed my desire to live and to be spared further pain above all other considerations.

But if I feared God's imminent judgment, I was even more afraid of the manner in which I would come to meet it. Most of all I feared what I might do between now and then: to what further depths of humiliation I would be willing to descend in what was bound to be a futile effort to save my life. Nothing in my recent performance led me to believe that I would die bravely or well.

My time, moreover, was running out. The parochial house was a large one that had once accommodated a parish priest, two curates, and a live-in housekeeper. Be-cause of the drop-off in vocations, my rapist was now the lone priest in residence, and the housekeeper came in only during daylight hours. She usually showed up at eight or so. Well before then, the priest out of sheer self-preservation would surely have to finish me off. I thought he would either beat me to death, or strangle me as he had done previously that night. I was especially afraid of the second possibility. Contrary to what I had always supposed, I learned that strangulation hurts atrociously—not so much where I thought it might, at the base of the throat, but at the side of the neck, radiating down into the shoulder. (The pain lasts a very long time before finally fading away. I wasn't right for months afterward.) The prospect of worse suffering before it was all over was un-endurable. My mind raced over the ghastly possibilities, though I was unable to make myself hang onto a single thought for more than a second.

My rapist decided that we should transfer the scene of operations back to the living room. He wanted a drink. Dragging me with him, he thrust me into a fireside chair and helped himself to a bottle and a glass. His fury was unabated and he stood over me, red-faced, continuing from a range of a very few inches to favor me with his as-tonishingly comprehensive views on my flaws of charac-ter, my arrogance, my holier-than-thou attitude, above all my betrayal of the affection and concern he had showered upon me, only to be greeted with ingratitude and con-tempt. He became more agitated and uncontrolled with each passing minute. His features grew distorted, flecks of whiskey-flavored spittle striking my face. It appeared to me that he was working himself up to the final crescendo of violence with which he would put an end to my life. When that moment came, I thought that I would try to make a break for the door. The key was still in the lock, needing only to be turned, but the deadbolts at the top and bottom were also secured. I had little expectation of being able to get all three opened in time.

The rant continued. After some time its focus broadened from me to other targets: the Church, the hierarchy, the contemptible and cowardly younger generation for which he had such hopes but that was failing to live up to them. Dredging up some piece of newspaper wisdom about what one is supposed to do in a kidnap situation, I went along with everything he said. Yes, Father. I entirely agree, Father. Can I go into the kitchen and make you something, Father? Anything to keep him talking. I didn't seriously imagine that he would completely forget the clock and continue like this until daybreak. But there was no harm in trying, even if it was certain to fail. All I truly hoped would come of stalling was to give him less time to dispose of my body, so that somebody, at least, would know what had become of me.

Keeping him engaged, trying to distract his attention from the passage of time, was a torture in itself. The tirade went on and on, I thought for hours, though it can't have been more than two at the outside. He was bitter, spiteful, profane, self-pitying, and endlessly repetitive. There was danger in contradicting him, but danger also, I found, in being too obsequious and open to persuasion.

Weakness roused his ire, redrawing it upon myself. Above all, he must not be allowed to lapse into silence, when murderous ideas might occur to him. And so we continued, while the inside of my head sang like a kettle. An interjection here. A question there. Yes, you're right, Father, but what about . . . ? It seemed as though the night would never end.

And then quite suddenly it did. The room was freezing cold, the curtains still tightly drawn and the electric lights burning. I sat on the edge of an armchair to the left of the empty fireplace. He was hunched in its twin on my right, a large glass-topped coffee table between us. He clutched his tumbler with both hands, an open half-bottle of whiskey thrust into the gap between the cushion of his chair and the side panel for easy replenishment. His speech had been getting slower for some time, a little more slurred. He was no longer looking at me. Finally the monologue stopped. I prodded him with a leading question. No answer. Another.

He raised his head and turned it in my direction.

"Go on."

A nod in the direction of the door. I rose to my feet, not sure whether it was a trick, trying to suppress the enormous, expanding bubble of incredulous optimism rising within me. Dear God in Heaven, if he only means it! Walk, don't run, nothing to provoke him. The quickest of surreptitious over-the-shoulder glances: was he getting up to stop me? No. Draw back the deadbolts—quietly!— now turn the key in the lock.

I opened the door, quickly stepped through, and closed it. On my left, within arm's length, was the wooden hat stand on which I had left my coat the previous evening. Without breaking stride I scooped it up and clattered down the stairs, taking them three and four at a time. No footsteps followed me. I opened the heavy Georgian outer door and slammed it behind me. In five seconds I was out on the street, where a few pedestrians were already taking the morning air.

It was ten minutes to eight on Saturday, the twenty-seventh of February. The whole attack had taken four hours, from start to finish.

3

On Doing the Right Thing

<hr>

IT IS A TRUTH UNIVERSALLY ACKNOWLEDGED, TO COIN A
phrase, that a binding moral obligation rests upon rape
victims to report their assaults and thereby ensure that
perpetrators do not go on to hurt anyone else.

So it seemed to me, at any rate. I didn't quite know
why I was still alive, but I was. For a few minutes I was
more gloriously happy than I had ever been in my life.
The euphoria was indescribable. The past four hours had
been my rapist's time, but this was mine. Now he would
answer for what he had done to me. Quite apart from
that, I had knowledge that a dangerous man was on the
loose. Many of my friends spent time in his company.

I should do something about it, and I was damn well going to.

But not right away. At that moment all I wanted to do was to sit and think for a while. There was a police station on the very same street as the parochial house, less than a mile to the north. First I turned east, toward the seafront where there was a small park with a public toilet. I wanted to see myself in the mirror.

Nothing prepared me for what I found. My neck felt as though it had swollen to about twice its previous girth. Swallowing hurt; turning my head hurt; everything hurt. Yet when I inspected myself, everything looked incomprehensibly normal. I moved closer. Some red marks and scratches at the base below the Adam's apple, yes, but nothing that couldn't have been done by a carelessly handled razor. Anxiously I popped open the first few buttons on my shirt and peered within. Some blotches here, a few shadows that looked as though they *might* develop into bruises there, but not the garish Coriolanian lesions I was sure I would find to testify to the nature of what I had just experienced.

> O, he is wounded; I thank the gods for't.
>   So do I too, if it be not too much; brings a'
> victory in his pocket? the wounds become him.

Mine did not become me. I probed further, in disbelief. It did not seem possible that so overwhelming an attack could have left so little physical trace. Above my right ear I found a large, tender swelling, quite obvious to the touch. It seemed to be filled with some kind of fluid. That was something, anyway. My eyes were deeply bloodshot. I looked as though I had smoked all the marijuana in the world. But, taken all in all, I was undeniably a going concern. I had looked worse, many times, coming off the pitch after a schools' kickabout.

Until that moment it had never even occurred to me that I might not be believed as soon as I disclosed what had happened to me. Now I wondered whether there was a reason why anyone should. Like a pricked bubble, my mood of elation vanished. My course of action as I fled the parochial house had seemed obvious. I could not imagine what had impelled the priest to make so monumental a blunder as to leave me free to give evidence against him, but that was his problem. I would make myself presentable at the park, go directly to the police station, and tell my story. Within an hour he would be leaving the parochial house in a squad car and (I devoutly hoped) handcuffs. Perhaps I would be taken to the hospital for a checkup. I would make a statement, though already I was thinking about what shaming details I might be able to leave out of it. It would all be very embarrassing but justice would be done.

Standing before the mirror I began to realize that it was unlikely to be as simple as that. How could I explain to the police the holes in my story that, the more I looked at it, seemed to be positively riddled with them? So you were invited to this social occasion. Did anybody see you there? Yes, yes, your friends; you mentioned that. Did any of them witness the assault? Oh, they left, did they? Why didn't you leave with them? Ah, he was drinking, of course. Not drunk enough that he wasn't able to overpower you, no, a fine young lad like yourself. All by himself, too. Hmm. And you lay down on the bed beside him. Did he force you do that too? He didn't, you say?

Sorry, what was that name you gave me again?

I did not go to the police station. I went outside and sat down on one of the children's swings. It was very cold. I could see my breath, but for some reason the chill didn't bother me as it usually does. Or perhaps I was too tired to shiver.

Nobody can accuse me of being excessively quick on the uptake. But I came to understand that the priest had not freed me in error. He had let me go because he knew I could do no harm to him.

And as I thought about it, I realized that he was right. I was a recent school-leaver, just beginning a blue-collar job. He was a pillar of the community, the very embodiment not just of respectability, but of sanctity. This was a very different time and place, well before the revelations of priestly abuse, before the wearing of a clerical collar in public became the nearest thing to a confession of guilt. Men of God stood on social pedestals—often disliked, sometimes mocked, but rarely openly opposed. Priests caught driving drunk got a quiet word and a police escort home, not a summons to the magistrates' court. It was an open secret that their tax returns went unquestioned by the revenue authorities. If their behavior became truly outrageous, representations were made to the episcopal palace, not the director of public prosecutions. My word against his. How far would that go?

There was a further consideration. I didn't know much about the law, but I was aware that homosexual acts (curiously, not lesbian ones) were still illegal, both in public and in private, under a Victorian-era antisodomy statute. The prohibition was rarely enforced. But it raised the stakes. Being, as the law said, a "male person," I was to confess before a law-enforcement officer that I had taken part in "the commission of an act of gross indecency with another male person," the maximum penalty for which was two years' imprisonment. My excuse to escape that punishment would be that I was acting under duress. What if the excuse was not accepted? If I could not persuade the police that I had been coerced, where would it leave me? Might my rapist and I both find ourselves behind bars? Or even . . . but surely that was too bizarre to consider.

I remained in the park for a long time: a couple of hours, I think. Then I walked to the square where I had left my motorbike the previous evening, unchained it, gingerly maneuvered the helmet onto my head, and drove slowly home.

.　.　.

I wasn't willing to leave things there. My friends were still at risk. Anyway, or so I told myself, I didn't really want to see my assailant in a prison cell. He needed to be locked up all right, but some institution where they would fit him out in something fetching in white with sleeves that tied at the back, and fix whatever short circuit in his wiring was making him act in this way, would do quite as well. As long as he was separated from the community, I could consider my duty done.

I was lying to myself, of course. Though I was perfectly correct, as later experience would prove, to conclude that there was nothing to be obtained from the police, I wanted an easier way out. The state might have no incentive to take me seriously, but the Church obviously did. It would be bound to take action, if only in its own self-interest.

My mother was at home. In those days I alternated between my parents' place on the weekends, and my sister's, just around the corner from my place of work, during the week. I asked my mother if she knew of a reliable, trustworthy priest: somebody with a level head who could give me advice on a knotty question. She was a member of several Catholic organizations, and far more plugged in to the religious scene than I was. After thinking for a moment, she gave me the name of a Capuchin friar attached to a large city-center church. She asked no questions, as was her way, and I volunteered no details. I telephoned the priory and made an appointment to see him the following day. Then I lay down for a few hours; slept; and got up for work.

I felt surprisingly normal as I did my usual rounds: clock-in at a quarter to ten; main gates closed at ten sharp; gatehouse entrance secured at half past; first patrol at eleven. Everything was quiet, as it nearly always was. A few late partygoers came in shortly after midnight, shhh-ing one another and giggling alcoholically as they went off to bed, their high heels clattering noisily along the corridors. I had four hundred students, most of them older than I, for whose safety I was theoretically responsible between ten at night and seven the following morning. It seemed ironic that they were relying on me, or at any rate paying me, to protect them from harm when I was unable to protect myself. But I was reassured, as I checked doors and windows and peered into the dark recesses of the campus, to discover that there were no lasting ill effects from my ordeal. Actually, I was doing pretty well. Perhaps I was making too big a deal out of the whole thing.

The following day, after again checking my body for bruises—infuriatingly, the ones below my breast-bone now seemed to be coming along nicely, and there was a large contusion over my right hip I hadn't even noticed the previous day—I visited the Capuchin friar in his office. He was a tall, lanky man of about fifty, with a straggly brown-and-white beard. Briefly I explained why I had come. He closed the door and motioned to me to continue. I spoke for five minutes or so about having been subjected to an "indecent assault," the most and least descriptive term I had been able to come up with, and my concern that the perpetrator would repeat his offense unless some action was taken. He frowned and nodded, pressing two fingers to his lips, staring at the desk between us and apparently concentrating deeply. When I had finished, he remained silent for some time. Finally he clapped his hands together and sat upright.

"All right," he said briskly. "I'm very glad you came to me with this. So, first things first. What I'm going to do now is to grant you Absolution."

"I'm sorry?"

"I'm going to absolve you. For the sins you may have committed with him. Your part in this. That's the most important thing you need. To be reassured of God's forgiveness, and I can give that to you right now. What you've just told me counts as your confession; we don't have to go over it again." He pronounced the words of absolution over me and gave me some token penance: two or three Hail Marys.

"Now," he went on, "what I want you to do is to leave this in my hands. We do see this kind of case from time to time, although it's very rare. But we take it very seriously indeed. I think I can promise you that neither you nor your friends will have any further difficulty from this man. Will you do that for me? Good. And don't hesitate to come back if there's anything else troubling you." He showed me to the door; saw me outside; and with a final wave and a "God bless you!" closed it again.

I stared at the door. The Capuchin had never asked me for the name of the priest who attacked me, nor had I mentioned it in his office. Later that evening I telephoned him again and reminded him of the fact. He apologized for his lapse of memory, and assured me that he would have contacted me the following day if I had not already called him.

The picture was beginning to become clearer. During the next week, before heading off to work I made the rounds of some of my old schoolmates, the ones who had not been in the parochial house that evening. It cut badly into my sleep time, and I found myself nodding off in my chair on the job between patrols. The conversations I initiated with them started with the usual lighthearted stuff, but before long were steered around to the topic of priests, altar boys, and so forth. It wasn't long before I started getting the answers I was looking for.

"Oh God, *him*?" one said. "You mean you don't know about him?"

"What then?"

"Buggered his own cousin. Poor kid was just fifteen or so. His old dear wanted to kick up a stink with the cops, but the rest of the family said no."

Additional stories followed. Some about gropings; hands thrust down trousers or up between legs; forced French kisses; bear hugs in doorways that went on for an inordinately long time. Others about consensual sexual relationships with boys and young men. All featuring alcohol. It seemed as though I was practically the only one in our circle who hadn't had a clue.

Anyway, I had the information I wanted. A week after my rape, I composed a short letter to the archbishop of the diocese, informing him of what had happened to me and that I was by no means the only one. The archbishop responded with an even briefer missive, courteously declining to get involved, but inviting me to discuss the matter with a senior diocesan official if I was so inclined.

I was, although I knew the score pretty well by now. It was in a spirit more of curiosity than expectation that I set up another appointment, at the parish in the south-city suburbs to which the official was attached. He turned out to be an elderly monsignor, desiccated in appearance and clearly nobody's fool. He spoke precisely, shortly, and to the point, like a first-rate trial lawyer, all the while saying nothing that could have caused him any embarrassment if published in the daily papers. In the elegant dining room to which he led me, he placed me on his right at the long, highly polished table while taking the chair at the end, with its back to the window, for himself. The evening light fell on my face; I could not see his. It occurred to me that thus far he had not missed a single trick.

The monsignor had a slim manila file in front of him, with my name on the cover. Evidently somebody had been making inquiries. He began by asking me to pray with him. I did. Then followed a series of questions on my religious practices and observances; views on certain theological and doctrinal controversies of the day; attitudes toward the Church. It seemed that the monsignor was trying to determine whether I was a sufficiently orthodox member of the flock, *croyant et pratiquant*, or somebody out to cause a public scandal. I had no objection to this line of questioning and answered honestly.

Finally the monsignor asked me to describe the incident about which I had written the archbishop. I gave him much the same abbreviated account as I had provided the Capuchin—rape with most of the sex and violence left out—and emphasized that my attacker was a highly dangerous man, uncontrollable while in drink, and a particular menace to young people. I expressed special concern about my own group of friends, who had been visiting the parochial house for a long time and were likely to go on doing so unless immediate action was taken. The attack on me, I reminded him, had not been an isolated incident. The monsignor took notes.

"Thank you," he said at the end. "That's all very clear. I'll report this matter to my superiors." The interview was plainly over. I started to rise.

"Oh, just one thing," he added. I sat down again. "We'd like to have some sort of ongoing line of communication about Father—what he's doing, whether he's drinking again, the people around him, and so forth. Would you be able to keep us up to date, when you see him again? A periodic report. It could be sent directly to me."

When I see him again? I tried to keep my voice steady, without success. "I don't think you understand, Monsignor. The man attacked me. He indecently assaulted me. There's no question of my having any further contact with him. I never want to see him again, in this life or the next."

The monsignor seemed disappointed. "Very well, if that's how you feel about it. I thought I'd ask." I picked up my motorcycle helmet and saw myself out.

. . .

That was the end of my career as a whistleblower. I put the word out among my circle of friends that the priest was a dangerous and abusive alcoholic, and that I had personal knowledge to back up that assessment. So far as I am aware, none of them heeded the warning, and soon I heard that the weekend parties at the parochial house had resumed.

That summer I sat the entrance exams for university, and in due course received a letter saying that I had obtained a place along with a small government scholarship. I gave notice at my job and sold my motorcycle to get enough money to pay the bills for the first year. Shortly before I started college, I heard from one of the old gang—I didn't see them much anymore; we seemed to have drifted apart—that there was a vacancy in the parochial house. The priest, he said, had been sent to a retreat center in a neighboring country for six months, and wouldn't be coming back to the parish. Some sort of scandal had been brewing, it appeared, and the clerical authorities thought it wise to bundle him out of the jurisdiction until the heat died down.

I nodded and turned the conversation to other matters. I wasn't really interested any more.

4

On Being a Man

EXPECTATIONS HAVE ALWAYS BEEN HIGH FOR RAPE VICTIMS, much more so than for those who have attacked them. Lucretia, daughter of a Roman consul, killed herself after her rape at sword point in 508 BC, and while Livy says that her family protested that she didn't need to do it to restore her honor, they don't seem to have tried very hard to stop her. Quintilian notes that the same standard applied to male victims, too, though in that situation, he helpfully reminded his readers, the rapist had an obligation to make things right with the bereaved family by paying them ten thousand sesterces. It's hardly surprising that self-destruction should have become the socially approved course of action for rape victims to follow, because it ticked off so many boxes. It definitively established, in a way that nothing else could do, that an actual rape had occurred, because nobody who had "really wanted it" would regard the sacrifice of their life as a reasonable price to pay for a moment's sexual gratification. It responded to the undoubted desire of some victims no longer to go on living. In a perverse way it acknowledged the gravity of rape, by treating the body and mind of the victim as having been damaged beyond repair. Most important of all, it relieved those in the suicide's immediate circle of the upsetting and awkward experience of being confronted by a person in distress who could not be comforted.

The attraction of suicide as a solution for the inconvenient problem posed by the existence of rape victims has never entirely faded. Even in societies in which this method of redressing the moral order has fallen into disuse, however, cultural demands are still rigorous. The victim of rape must provide acceptable proof of nonconsent, nonculpability, and nongullibility; assume responsibility for preventing the attacker from committing future crimes (or, through failing to report the rape, accept a share of the guilt for those crimes); pass through the appropriate stages of trauma, minimization, reorganization, and renormalization in an orderly and timely manner; and emerge from the experience a better and stronger person, symbolized by the abandonment of the passive and stig-matizing status of victim in favor of that of survivor.

It's a daunting list, and it's just as well that I was not required to conform to these requirements, as I would al-ready have miserably failed to meet most of them. Fortu-nately they didn't apply to me, as I was not a rape victim. Having put my "attack" firmly behind me, I was ready to proceed directly to the ultimate stage of getting on with my life. It's true that I was concerned for months after-ward about the possibility that I might have contracted a sexually transmitted disease, though wild horses would not have dragged me to a doctor even if I had begun to display symptoms. And granted, there were one or two things from which I found it convenient to steer clear (books and articles about rape, incest, or sexual assault; certain scenes in films or television programs, of which there seemed more with each passing year, because in fact there were; particular aromas; various pieces of music; the dark; drunk people; anything around my neck; people coming up behind me; people hugging me without my consent; people touching me for any reason at all . . .), but on the whole I was good to go. I felt perfectly fine, or so I believed. At the time, I didn't know the difference between that and not feeling anything at all.

University seemed to be just what the doctor ordered. Enrolling in an unarmed-combat class, I spent two nights

a week throwing my fellow students across the gymna-
sium and being thrown in my turn, breaking several un-
important bones in the course of my training but boosting
my self-confidence greatly. I found new friends to replace
my old ones, with whom I had almost entirely lost touch.
The coursework was absorbing and extremely demand-
ing. Having gone to a terrible secondary school, I discovered many deficiencies in my academic preparation,
especially in foreign languages. I worked all the hours God
sent, as did the majority of my fellow students. Romantic
pressures were few—our nickname for the place was "the
Monastery," only partly a reference to its ancient origins
on the site of an Augustinian abbey—which suited me
down to the ground. We were bright, ambitious, industri-
ous, and perpetually broke. Summers were spent abroad,
taking seasonal jobs in food processing or at coastal resort towns to earn enough to keep us going through the
following academic year. I did well in my exams, and was
encouraged by my tutors to begin preparing for doctoral
work as soon as I completed my undergraduate studies.

In reality I was building castles upon sand, though
neither I nor anybody else realized it at the time. Warning
signs were not lacking. My sleep was badly disrupted. It
had been a standing joke in my family that I could drop
off almost instantly while lying on wet cobblestones, but
now things were very different. I slept lightly, fitfully,

and only with the lights on, a habit I wouldn't succeed in breaking until comparatively recently. Nightmares were disturbing and relentless. Eventually I found it easier to work through the night and snatch a few hours' rest between dawn and my first lectures, a pattern of behavior that undergraduate life accommodated readily enough. More seriously, my weight began to melt away. I wasn't anorexic in the classic sense. I'd always been a stringbean, more apt to drop the pounds than put them on. I attached no particular value to being thin, and felt no compunction about eating as much as I wanted at mealtimes. The difficulty was that these days I didn't seem to want very much at all. I often forgot to eat, and although this regime did enable me to conform my living expenses to my straitened budget, photographs from that time show that I had become gaunt and wasted to an alarming degree.

It didn't take very much finally to push me over the edge. Toward the end of my third year of studies, the father of one of my secondary-school friends died, and I went to attend the funeral mass. We hadn't seen each other for a long time—he'd had a short stint in a seminary, dropped out, and was now studying law—and while waiting for the ceremony to begin, we squatted in the church vestibule and got caught up on our lives as he chain-smoked his way through half a packet of cigarettes. While we were talking, a shadow fell across us. I glanced up, and saw my rapist standing almost at my feet, staring down at me.

The years seemed to have been kind to him. His face was filled out a little and he had color in the cheeks; he looked fit and well rested. Several clerical friends were with him. He did not speak, nor did I. He scrutinized me for a few seconds, drew his face into a sneer, then turned abruptly and marched into the church with his party. He was to be the officiant. I followed automatically with all the others and found a seat at the back.

I'm not sure what I did the rest of that day. I know I visited my sister's flat on the other side of town. When she returned from work that evening, she found me sitting on her kitchen floor in the middle of a large puddle of Coca-Cola from a bottle that I had let fall, crying so hard that I could not speak or respond to her questions. Astutely divining that all was not well, she telephoned for help. Within a couple of hours I had been admitted to a center-city psychiatric hospital.

The processing was long and complicated, which at least gave me an opportunity to pull myself together. I saw a female psychiatrist, then a male one, then a male charge nurse. Each questioned me as to the nature of my problem. I told them that I was upset because three years previously I had been sexually assaulted—if the "r" word was still beyond me, I could by now manage the "s" one—by a priest, and had recently seen him again. On all three occasions this abruptly stopped the conversation. Finally I was given a bed and a tranquillizer pill, which brought on a drugged sleep.

The following morning, in borrowed pajamas and dressing gown, I was taken to see the deputy head of the department. He was a brusque, jowly man in his forties, wearing a brown tweed jacket and with the demeanor of an impatient middle-ranking bureaucrat. He spent some minutes reading the notes from the admissions staff while I sat in silence opposite him, before asking what was the matter with me.

I started to explain about the sexual assault. He cut me off in midsentence. "Look," he said, "I don't want to hear any of that. I'm not interested in what kind of stories you're telling yourself. You're here because you can't cope with your problems. And you're not going to get better until you start coming to terms with your homosexuality."

"I'm not homosexual."

"Do you have a girlfriend?"

"No, I don't."

"Have you ever had any sexual experience with a girl?"

"No."

He threw down his pencil in a gesture of exaspera-
tion. An hour later I was transferred to a "locked ward,"
a six-bed unit where the patients were not permitted to
have access to any other part of the hospital. The other
beds were already filled, a couple of them with elderly
men suffering from chronic alcoholism. The nurses too
were males, hefty individuals in T-shirts who looked like
nightclub bouncers. I was promised an appointment with
the hospital's resident "psychosexual expert." Unfortunately he had departed overseas for a fortnight's summer
holiday and I would have to await his return.

The purpose of placing me on this ward, it appeared,
was to force me into association with the patient in the
bed beside mine, a bipolar young man of about eighteen
who had attempted suicide by cutting his wrists. I did not
find him aggressive or menacing, but he was extremely
persistent. He had a single topic of conversation, his recent discovery that he was gay, and, being in the manic
phase of his illness, he was burning to compare notes
with me. I couldn't think of anything to say that was
relevant to his situation, and found his endless questions
and suggestions exhausting. After three days of this, having slept neither day nor night, I decided that if I was
not already genuinely insane, I would soon become so.
My mother, who visited me, was of the same opinion.

Unwilling to wait any longer for the psychosexual expert to materialize, she signed me out of the hospital against medical advice.

.   .   .

Fortunately I had timed my mini-breakdown for a convenient stage in the academic year. The summer vacation began a few days later and, having had an offer of three months' temporary work abroad, I departed in the belief that a change of scene could only do me good.

In fact it made no difference. The essence of the problem was that until this point, having an abundance of youthful energy, I had been able to dedicate a great deal of it to the arduous task of constructing and maintaining an edifice of denial of how deeply I had been harmed by my experience. That reservoir was now exhausted. My rapist's reappearance on the scene certainly hadn't helped, but in hindsight it's clear that I was heading for a smash sooner rather than later.

After returning home, I prepared for my final year of college. I no longer attended lectures or tutorials, at first because I feared I would break down in tears and cause an embarrassing scene if I became drawn into conversation with another person on any subject at all. Later, I simply didn't have the energy for anything but the most superficial social interactions, such as paying for groceries at the supermarket. I kept to my off-campus residence for almost the entire year, writing my essays and papers at the library of another college across town where I could be sure of not meeting anybody I knew. Most of my friends believed that I had dropped out of university. I acquired the means of self-destruction, and drew comfort from the knowledge that they were available to me whenever I might need them. In all likelihood I was clinically depressed.

One day my eye fell on a small paragraph in the newspaper reporting that the local rape crisis center had decided to begin accepting calls from male victims of sexual abuse. I carried the clipping around for many weeks before deciding to call. I'm ashamed to say that I behaved very badly when I first tried to do so. The "hello" at the other end aroused a deep unreasoning panic in me; I could not speak and I must have put the telephone down on the poor woman half a dozen times in twenty minutes without saying a word. Eventually I managed a strangled "hello" of my own, and she kindly refrained from admonishing me as I deserved.

I believe I was the first, or one of the first, adult men the organization had ever encountered. Like most rape crisis centers then and now, it was a private, voluntary body, though funded in part by the government. All the staff were women, and their counseling philosophy was influenced by the work of several American feminist scholars, notably Susan Brownmiller and Diana Russell. Rape, in this view, was best understood as a political act rather than a crime committed by abnormal individuals, its function and intent being to sustain a much larger edifice of male privilege and female subordination permeating every aspect of life. Whether they were themselves rapists or not, all men derived benefits from this overarching system of oppression, and were thus implicated in it.

The logic of this argument, from which my counselors did not shy away, was that the existence of rape in some respects served my interests also, and that it would not be unreasonable for me to regard myself as having been to some extent hoisted by my own petard. As a topic for academic debate, it could have been potentially stimulating; in a therapeutic setting, it carried more than a whiff of victim blaming. The same could be said of one of the earliest questions put to me: whether I had committed sexual abuse in the past or was currently doing so. This was my first exposure to the "vampire syndrome" theory—the unfounded, but still astonishingly prevalent, supposition that a male victim of sexual crime, like people bitten by Count Dracula, is much more likely to develop into an abuser himself. A less insensitive but still somewhat tone-deaf philosophy underlay my counselor's initial explanation for my inability to come to terms with what had happened to me. Males who had experienced sexual abuse, she told me, could no longer perceive themselves as superior to women, because they had been treated as women often are. What they were mourning was as much the loss in their own eyes of the inflated social status men routinely assume in patriarchal society as the trauma of the actual assault.

At the time, I possessed neither the vocabulary nor the confidence to question this framing of my own rape. It struck me as bizarre nonetheless that anyone would suppose that of all the reasons for a person to be disturbed by having undergone a violent sexual attack, this one would feature at or near the top of the list. But in fact I was simply running up against what I later found to be the nearest thing to a universal law, regardless of one's sex, age, or race: when a person is raped, everybody else knows better than the victim why it happened and what it really means. Only the nature of the explanation differs, according to whom one asks.

My counseling was not a success, but not primarily for that reason. I believe that the staff at the center genuinely meant well, even though they seemed to find it impossible to conceptualize what rape might mean for men without first translating it into categories that were more familiar to them. No body of scholarship or accumulation of practical knowledge existed to guide them as to how male victims typically responded or should be treated;

like me they were groping in the dark for answers. In fairness to them, the number of suggestions made to me that I cope with the assault by problematizing my own masculinity diminished rapidly over time, no doubt as they saw how much distress I was in. And the fault for my lack of progress was almost entirely my own. Rarely can they have dealt with a less articulate client. I would arrive for a counseling session, soak my way through half a box of their Kleenex, be reduced to tongue-tied confusion by questions like "How are you feeling?," and leave in a greater state of agitation than when I had arrived. The ergonomics of the room weren't good—if anyone has in it in mind to set up a service catering to men, they will get far better results by wearing out some shoe leather while walking in the open air with their clients than wedging them into the corner of an office, especially if the counselor should then position him- or herself between the client and the door. In the end, though, it was a case of the blind leading the blind. I was unable to put my experiences or my feelings into words, and the people at the center didn't know the correct ones to lend to me.

The end of my time at university was fast approaching. I told my counselor that I would be leaving the country permanently as soon as I graduated, and thought that the time had come to discontinue attending the center. She agreed that this would be a good idea.

I found these attempts to disclose what had happened to me to be almost unbearably painful, not much less so than the rape itself. I was a walking anomaly: I had been raped, but I was not a woman, not a child, not a prison inmate, not gay, and not a perpetrator. At the time, the number of such people was authoritatively stated to be so insignificant that little needed to be said or thought about them, and consequently almost nothing was. (On one occasion, a particularly ideologically engaged volunteer at the center—admittedly, one regarded even by her colleagues as an outlier—told me that if I wanted to prove I genuinely cared about the problem of rape, I would choose to remain silent so as not to distract attention from the real victims.) Books and scholarly articles took it for granted that the only type of sexual crime worth mentioning consisted of the kind involving male perpetrators and female victims; even the very large number of prison rapes that everybody agreed were occurring were mostly ignored in the literature. I felt very alone, and saw nothing to indicate that "coming out" in any setting was or ever would be a realistic proposition, far less a safe one. The best thing I could do in the circumstances, it seemed to me, was to take the outlier-volunteer's advice and say nothing to anyone about what had happened to me. And I have not, from that day to this one.

.   .   .

Rape is a gendered crime, but not in the sense in which that term is conventionally used. There's no disputing that it is perpetrated against particular kinds of human bodies, and minds that have been shaped by the experience of living in those bodies. As a man, my rape did not expose me to some of the consequences I would have faced had I been a woman, including but by no means limited to the risk of pregnancy. As a heterosexual, my later experiences of sexual intimacy do not resemble the events of that night to anything like the same degree that they would if I had been gay. Any number of similar examples could be cited.

I'd be the last person in the world to claim that gender makes no difference. Obviously it did to me, and in ways that did not always serve to mitigate or reduce the painfulness of the experience. To be a man who has been raped gives rise to unique problems, though not all men will encounter them in the same forms or process them in the same way. The range of normal male responses to sexual victimization, like female ones, is very wide indeed.

The first problem, of course, is establishing that he has been raped at all. Women are already very familiar with that dilemma, and to escape it must satisfy a rigorous set of criteria. To qualify as having experienced a "true rape" (or what Whoopi Goldberg charmingly describes as "rape-rape"), a woman must have been attacked (i) by a stranger; (ii) in a well-trafficked, public place; (iii) while decorously dressed; (iv) without having consumed alcohol or other mood-altering substances; (v) after physically as well as verbally resisting (bonus points for torn clothing and photogenic injuries); and (vi) in such a manner as will enable her to provide an accurate and prompt description of the assailant to the police.

In their way, the requirements for the male victim are no less stringent. He must be attacked by several assailants, not just one, for to permit himself to be overpowered by a single attacker represents culpable failure on his part and itself goes a long way to explain, if not actually to justify, his assault. Not only must he physically resist, but he must continue to do so until beaten to the point of insensibility or death. The forms of his rape must not require any activity on his part (e.g., manual or oral stimulation of his attackers) that might give rise to awkward questions about the unwillingness of his participation. He must not be in prison unless, like the hero of *The Shawshank Redemption*, he is able to establish definitively his innocence of any crime. He must be heterosexual, but must also not display any involuntary physiological response to the attack: neither erection nor, above all, ejaculation. Afterward, he must personally assume responsibility for visiting an equivalent level of non-sexual violence upon his attackers, without involving or even notifying the authorities of the original crime. This accomplished, he must quickly return to a state of full physical, psychological, and psychosexual functioning—preferably without therapeutic intervention of any kind, but at most after a short and discreet period of treatment. (In romantic fiction, the love of a good woman can serve as a cost-effective substitute for expensive engagements with the health services.) Lastly, he must never afterward speak of his victimization to anyone.

This may seem like a caricature, and of course it is. But it is in my experience all too typical of the expectations of men and women alike for male rape victims. Because of the virtual impossibility of anyone actually being able to satisfy all or most of these conditions, men who have been raped find that their silence is rigorously socially policed. Insistence upon the rarity of male rape serves the same function, ensuring the nonexistence of any specialized infrastructure or body of knowledge that would enable the caricature to be tested against, and modified by, lived reality. That's why, on those vanishingly rare occasions a man does speak up about being raped, a thing he is likely to fear even more than that he will not be believed, is that he will be.

A second and closely related problem is the absence of a vocabulary that can simultaneously accommodate the existence of concepts of masculinity (as something other than a social problem to be rectified) and the fact that men are, not infrequently, raped or otherwise sexually abused. Much of our difficulty in this respect derives from the confusion of metaphorical and descriptive language when discussing rape. My counselor's insistence that what I resented above all about my own assault was being subjected to a form of forced feminization is a textbook example. Perhaps it was true that having been raped did make me feel less "male," whatever she or anyone else might understand by that term. But even if so, it did not in fact make me feel more "female"—any more than being forced to participate in a sex act with a man would in and of itself cause me to regard men as more desirable sexual partners. No doubt what she really meant to say was that I could now better understand—without actually sharing in—one of the defining elements of living in a woman's body, the condition of sexual vulnerability. If so, I take the point, though I would personally wish to add that rape is neither an ethical nor an effective method of teaching empathy. But in general, outside the context of the gender wars, this kind of language is thoroughly unhelpful. Men, straight or gay, who are raped are not *literally* feminized; they must and will continue to live in the world, in a man's body, and participate in a society that for better or worse will remain gender based (however fluid those categories may become in the future). To suggest that they translate what happened to them into preexisting categories of analysis devised for an entirely different purpose, with different meanings, is simply a way of refusing to take their experience seriously and on its own terms. If it turns out that those terms do not yet exist, then they need to be formulated. It is for the victims alone to decide what they ought to be.

Not all components of rape or sexual assault, moreover, and possibly not even the most important ones, are bound up with the particularities of gender. Bodily violation, physical suffering, being put in fear of one's life—these, and many other things, are common factors that are typically experienced in very much the same ways, regardless of whether the victim is male, female, or transgender; gay, straight, or asexual. Subdividing rape into innumerable categories—"classic" rape, date rape, war rape, male rape, child rape, female-on-female rape, etc.—other than to provide specialized services responding to people's individual needs carries many more costs than benefits. In the competition for resources and public awareness, it gives rise to a kind of "victimhood Olympics" in which each group tries to prioritize its claims against all the others, to the detriment of the whole. (I readily acknowledge that in that competition, my own experience does not place me any higher than, let us say, fourteenth or fifteenth at best. The problem is that in the victimhood Olympics, even the fourteenth- and fifteenth-place finishers also receive a prize.) Much more seriously, it generates a dynamic in which the many particular kinds of rape, and the actually existing people victimized by them, are transformed into anomalies, and erased from view by being contrasted against some imagined norm.

In the end we are all human beings, and human beings who have been raped have the very devil of a time. It's important not to lose sight of that.

. . .

There's an endless debate over whether rape is about sexual gratification on the one hand, or a display of power and dominance on the other: sex accomplished violently, or violence accomplished sexually. It may be a meaningful question in the context of figuring out the mind-set of perpetrators, but from the victim's perspective it probably doesn't matter very much. Whatever the attacker's motivations may be, it is almost impossible not to experience the episode as a targeted assault on one's sexual being. Unlike, say, a brawl in a pub in which the assailant doesn't care what he's hitting as long as he succeeds in putting his opponent on the floor, in a rape or other form of sexual assault particular parts of the body, particular organs, are singled out for attention. How one relates thereafter to other persons when these same elements of one's anatomy are part of the interaction is thus likely to become more complicated than in the past. This seems almost too obvious to point out, but as George Orwell usefully reminds us, "To see what is in front of one's nose requires a constant struggle."

I don't think I am more emotionally illiterate than the next man, though I'd never claim to be any less so. It's richly ironic, though, that until comparatively recently if you had asked me whether there had been any lasting sexual ramifications to my attack, I should have assured you with complete conviction that there was none whatever. Except if you ignored, as I did, the fact that I was eighteen when I was raped, and the next time I went on a date was when I was thirty-six.

The reason I'd have given such a self-evidently fatuous answer was that I would have interpreted the question narrowly. Did I have a physical sexual response—e.g., an erection—during my attack, and did that cause me difficulties regarding sexual intimacy in later life? The answer to the first part was "no," and hence, I assumed, the second didn't arise. This was, needless to say, all of a piece with my intense disinclination to address any element of what had occurred to me that wasn't clamoring for my immediate attention.

It ought to go without saying, but clearly doesn't, that responding physically to a sexual assault, whether through erection, lubrication, or orgasm, indicates precisely nothing about one's sexual identity or degree of consent. For men and women alike, such reactions may not be characteristic, but neither are they at all uncommon. Their *only* significance ought to be that attempts by rapists to elicit them in the hope of confusing the victim about the degree of coercion involved in the assault—as unfortunately successfully occurs in too many instances— should be considered an aggravating factor when passing sentence. Cats that have been seriously injured by farm machinery sometimes purr afterward. That doesn't mean they enjoyed it.

In my own case, I was spared the experience of having apparently been betrayed by my body, and this enabled me to believe that for me the rape had no adverse sexual consequences of any kind—the above-mentioned two decades of involuntary celibacy notwithstanding. The truth was far different, as I learned after I married. Most nights there were two people in our bedroom, but sometimes there were three. The fact that the interloper was occupying head-space in my brain, rather than bed-space in the physical realm did not make his presence any less real or disquieting. Trying to contrive matters so that nothing about our lovemaking should even by implication resemble what transpired in another bedroom, years earlier, while not shutting out my wife (or, worse, tipping my hand to her about my past) did not conduce to the light-hearted, playful attitude toward marital intimacy that I had always hoped to cultivate. Luckily the episodes have become less frequent over time, but whenever they occur, as regrettably they still do, they infallibly creep the hell out of me. These were the only occasions when the notion of going back home and killing my rapist didn't seem like such a terrible idea after all.

Most of the relatively sparse literature that exists on the subject of the rape of men tells me that anxiety or confusion over one's sexual identity is a typical response on the part of heterosexual victims. It may be so, for all I know, but I'm inclined to doubt that it's quite as prevalent, at any rate among those who were adults at the time of their rape, as expert opinion would have it. Perhaps I'm simply lacking in imagination. But the claim fits so neatly into prejudicial social scripts about "unmanning" and the "vampire syndrome"—in addition to us all becoming abusers through having been raped, seemingly our sexuality is overwritten by the same mysterious process—that it's hard to avoid a degree of skepticism.

If men are reluctant to disclose their experiences of sexual victimization, it seems to me, the principal reason is to be found not in internalized homophobia (which, if true, would presumably result in a higher rate of reporting by gay men, who do not appear to be less vulnerable to rape than anyone else) but in the cult of masculine stoicism that is encouraged, if not enforced, across the social and sexual spectrum. Whether exhorted to take their lumps uncomplainingly in the service of traditional conceptions of masculinity, or to check their privilege in the interest of undermining them, the net effect is the same. I confess to a degree of impatience with those who lament the limited emotional palette of men, offering it as an all-purpose explanation for the continuing stigma that surrounds questions of male sexual assault. It may indeed be a factor, but there are other more tangible ones also.

One wonders what would happen if all the men and boys who had experienced sexual victimization were to follow the well-meaning advice offered them and speak up at once. Based on my own experience, as well as that of others, I am not quite sure that as many people as is sometimes suggested would be ready to hear them.

5

On Not Getting Over It

THE ROOM IS DARK, THE CURTAINS DRAWN TIGHTLY AGAINST the street light. I am lying on top of the bed, fully clothed except for my shoes. I listen intently for the sound of deep, regular respirations that will tell me that the person stretched out on my right has dropped off to sleep, making it safe for me to leave. I have been in this room before. My heart is pounding at a furious rate and I am having difficulty controlling my breathing. I keep my upper body perfectly still, slowly inching my left leg over the side toward the floor. As my toes touch it, the bed frame, released from some of my weight, creaks loudly. I freeze. Several minutes later, I repeat the same delicate maneuver with my right leg and foot and, with exquisite caution, raise my entire body off the bed. Once upright I stand quietly in the darkness, scanning for any reaction. Hearing none, I take three long, rapid strides to the door, step quickly through, and close it behind me.

My wife is there in her cotton nightdress, returning from the bathroom. "That took a long time," she says.

"Yeah," I reply. "She wasn't too keen to get to sleep tonight."

"Well, that's four-year-olds for you," my wife sagely observes. She is shortsighted without her contact lenses, and squints blearily at me as she makes her way back to our bedroom. Abruptly she stops, an alarmed expression on her face.

"My God! What's the matter with you?"

"What do you mean?"

"Look at your shirt. You've sweated right through it. Are you coming down with something?"

"No, I'm fine. It was pretty hot in there. I cracked her window a while ago."

"All right . . . still, you'd better throw that one in the laundry basket. I'll wash it tomorrow."

My wife returns to bed. I peel the T-shirt damply off my back, pull it over my head, and towel myself off with it. In the medicine cabinet there is an old bottle containing five or six dusty Percocet tablets, the remnants of a dozen prescribed to me when I had root-canal surgery the previous year. I scan the label; the dose is the lowest possible. I swallow two of them and sit on the living room sofa, waiting for my heart to stop trying to hammer its way out of my chest. I am forty-six years of age.

The Greek word *trauma* means "wound." Contrary to the cant phrase, time does not heal all of them. The best I can say about my rape is that over the years I've achieved an uneasy modus vivendi with it, but one that is constantly threatening to break down and sometimes does so. In some respects I have "moved on with my life." I emigrated to the country where I now live, finished graduate school, and built a professional career. Complete physical separation not just from the scene of the crime but from anyone who previously knew me was a positive thing. It enabled me to set the boundaries for my interaction with others at levels that, for a long time, were the only ones I was capable of handling.

Granted, those boundaries were extremely narrow ones. For one thing, they precluded any kind of romantic involvement. Partly this was the result of my ongoing catastrophic difficulties with the idea of touching and being touched. Part of it was because I had little energy left over from the sometimes-overwhelming challenge of making it through the day. Mostly, though, it was a result of my inability to come up with an answer to the conundrum of how to handle my past in the context of a long-term relationship. The idea of disclosing it to a girlfriend was unthinkable. So was concealing it, if things were to move along in a more serious direction.

It wasn't until my mid-thirties that I felt ready at last to dip my toe into the dating pool. Eventually I fell in love with someone that I wanted to marry. With her, at least, physical contact no longer seemed an impossibility. But broaching the topic on my mind still was. While we were dating, she told me of some of the traumatic experiences in her own past which, while not sexual in nature, had clearly deeply affected her. It might have seemed like an obvious time to liberate the skeleton in my own closet. Instead, it made it more difficult. I didn't feel that I could mention my troubles without seeming to trivialize or one-up hers. The moment passed, and the problem remained unresolved.

The way I eventually handled it, once I'd made up my mind to propose to my fiancée-to-be, was an unsatisfactory compromise. I told her that there were some dark issues in my past that had been and were likely always to be troublesome; that I would probably never be able to talk about them; and that if I were to become quiet and withdrawn from time to time, this would be the reason. That formula, I know, left much to be desired. Starting a marriage with secrets kept from one's spouse is never a good idea. It was in some ways unfair to her, as it withheld the information necessary for her to assess just how big a problem she might be taking on by marrying me. There was an element of selfishness in it, too. I wanted her to think well of me, and was reluctant to disclose things that would lower me in her estimation.

And yet . . . I recoil from the notion of a hard-and-fast rule that rape victims have an obligation to tell potential spouses about what happened to them. For a significant proportion, myself included, it's simply impossible to speak of these things, however much they might want to. To make prior disclosure a requirement for marriage or other long-term relationships is in effect to foreclose those possibilities for them.

One thing is certain, though. There's never a good time, and waiting makes it more difficult rather than easier. A moment never arises in a marriage when you can get away with saying to your spouse, "Oh, by the way, love, I've been meaning to mention—somebody raped me when I was eighteen. Well, got to fly or I'll miss my bus. Don't forget to let the cat out." I go back and forth over this question, but my current thinking is that disclosure in a relationship is something that should happen early or not at all.

. . .

When I was younger, I used to fantasize about what "getting over" my rape would look like. At first I thought that simply knowing I wasn't the only person in the world to whom this had happened would be enough. The more I reflected upon it, though, the longer the list of requirements became. I wanted to have the option of coming out of the closet, to be able to speak about it to others without evoking derision, dismissal, incredulity, jocularity, or contempt. I wanted some kind of public acknowledgement, not necessarily from the criminal justice system (but there too if possible) that raping me was wrong, and that I was not the only one who resented it, or ought to. I wanted the innumerable forms of sexual victimization, and the appalling scale on which they occurred, to be addressed by state and society with the seriousness they deserved. I wanted my rapist to be forced to confront the reality of the harm he had done to me, and for him somehow to develop the moral capacity to appreciate it. I wanted the illusions that before the attack I had had about myself and about the world in which I lived to be restored. I wanted a great many things, none of which I was ever likely to get.

In the meantime, the ordinary business of life still had to be dealt with. Over the years, I evolved a way of adjusting expectations to realities. It was important, I decided, to recognize that some things were never going to get better. I should concentrate on restoring a measure of functionality to my life (for example, learning to sleep with the lights out, or suppressing the impulse to vomit whenever the dentist placed instruments inside my mouth) and let time take care of the rest.

This rough-and-ready method of partial adjustment has worked, more or less. The number of things that trigger serious distress in me has diminished. Going to the dentist is still something for which I have to psych myself up over a couple of days—an environment in which I lie flat on my back while someone looms above me, putting things in my mouth that I don't want there while causing me pain and making me gag, is a compendium of all the horrors, wrapped up in a neat little parcel. Fortunately, lots of people have dental anxiety, and my profuse sweating and habit of keeping my eyes tightly closed throughout the procedure attracts no particular attention. (As for the urologist . . . agh! don't get me started.) While I still don't like being touched without permission, I have overcome the strong desire to flatten whoever's doing it. To be sure, there are still a great many external stimuli that can make a mess of my day. Life as a rape victim, as they say, resembles nothing so much as being a long-tailed cat in a roomful of rocking chairs. In general, though, anything that happens in the daylight hours I can handle.

The nights are a different story. Nightmares, or, as they're sometimes called, "rapemares"—powerful, vivid, and upsetting—started soon after the attack. They have remained a serious problem until the present day. The typical pattern is for me to drop off fairly quickly; experience in dreams some variation on an ugly theme that will jerk me back into wakefulness in a lather of muck-sweat; and then, after my pulse rate returns to normal, to resume sleep until morning. Sometimes, though, the disturbing images come so thick and fast that further rest is impossible. Thirty or forty nights a year I require a dose of cough syrup or one of my wife's allergy pills to get to sleep; fifteen or twenty more I don't sleep at all. These symptoms, I've learned, are not at all uncommon among people who have had similar experiences. The existing treatments available don't seem to make much of a difference, according to expert opinion, so I've never bothered to pursue them.

Most days are good, though quite a few aren't. Earlier on, I often found myself being overwhelmed by disturbing flashbacks and extended periods of sadness, sometimes lasting for weeks or months. With time I learned that the best thing to do was to ride the wave rather than struggle against it: to accept that I was going to be down for an indeterminate period and to concentrate on completing the most important daily tasks while that was happening. Nowadays I have a dozen or so of these slumps in the course of a year, normally lasting two or three days, but some continuing for longer. Thus far I haven't been able to identify what sets them off, how severe they'll be, or how long they'll continue. The important thing is knowing that they do come to an end.

This is the way I live now. It's not a bad life, taken as a whole. But it's very different from the one I had, and still more from the one I planned to have. Not every negative thing in my life has been a consequence of rape, nor would everything necessarily have been a bed of roses if it had never occurred. Nobody is guaranteed a safe or stable existence. Still, if I am honest with myself, I am compelled to acknowledge that being raped is the most consequential thing that has happened to me, the episode that has had by far the greatest impact. Had it not taken place, I would never have emigrated from my home country. I would not have subordinated any thought of a personal life to career development in what ultimately proved to be an inadequate coping strategy. Without it, I might have been spared the full awareness of radical evil in the world, and of my own response when confronted with it, both of which have had entirely destructive and negative effects. As Adam and Eve discovered in the garden, there are some kinds of knowledge that it is better never to have. My rape did not take away all the good things in life. There are moments of happiness with my wife and daughter; professional accomplishments from which I gain satisfaction; pastimes that interest and engage me. But it's taken away a hell of a lot.

.   .   .

Rape is loss. It deprives the victim of something vital, whose importance is only recognized when it is no longer there. The change is permanent and irreversible. That is a hard thing for anyone to accept, and especially difficult, perhaps, for men, whose way of being in the world does not sit comfortably with the idea of losses that can never be made good.

At present we lack an adequate vocabulary for speaking about loss. Our favored idioms are rather about the regaining of something that has been temporarily misplaced, or the restoration of something that is (always reparably) damaged. We are intensely ill at ease in the presence of anguish that cannot be relieved, and mourning that cannot be assuaged. We shy away from parents who have lost children, or cancer sufferers who are terminally ill, not because we do not feel for them in their pain, but because we quite literally do not know what to say.

People who have been raped are brought up constantly against these limits of language. I make my living through the use of words, yet I find myself as tongue-tied when speaking of such things as anyone else. The expressions

I want to use are melodramatic, hyperbolic, so much so that even to think them is embarrassing. Four unpleasant hours in an upstairs room is not like the death of a child. It is not like being a prisoner in a concentration camp. One feels selfish doing or saying anything that would in any sense seem to make a short-lived episode from which one was able to walk away comparable, however remotely, to sufferings so much greater than one's own.

Yet there is a truth in the melodrama that the rhetoric of "healing," "recovery," or "becoming a survivor" lacks for me, and that is its insistence that what I have lost is never coming back. This is something that I know to be true at the innermost core of my being. Parts of my personhood—the better parts—were severed in that room. What is left is still recognizably mine, and existed before the attack, but this remnant is now out of balance. I can add elements to it to try to make up the difference, and over the years have done so. But the result is a brittle composite that bears only a passing resemblance to what preceded it.

Almost all the changes are negative. I nearly said "all," because the idea of rape as *unmitigated* loss is also one that feels intuitively true to me. That wouldn't be strictly accurate, though. I have gained one thing out of the experience: a measure, however inadequate, of tolerance for the failings of others. Before this happened, I had all the makings of a fine young prig, with a highly developed and thoroughly inflexible sense of rectitude. Afterward, my moral compass may not have shifted dramatically, but I became far more conscious of everyone's need, and especially my own, for forgiveness rather than righteousness. When I do stand before the judgment seat of God, the only thing I expect to have to say, and the only thing likely to do me any good, is "Be merciful unto me, a sinner."

In every other respect, though, I am the worse for having gone through it. It was not a learning experience, a wake-up call, a trial by fire, or a challenge triumphantly overcome. Rather it was a forced exposure to the world as it really is. The veil that separates normal life from barbarity and horror is tissue-paper thin, and can be torn aside with shocking ease and a complete lack of warning. Dreadful things can and do happen, and having once happened can do so again. This seems like a truism until it is lived. Then it takes on a significance that colors every aspect of one's future life. It's not a question of being wary, or trusting fewer people, or looking for hidden dangers, though one does all those things. Nor is it even living in fear, because when one knows the thing to be feared, it loses most of its power to disturb. It's more a matter of anticipation, of living in a constant state of expectation for the next moment when oneself, or a loved one, will be dragged suddenly through the veil to the other side, to receive another hands-on lesson in the way things really are. As will surely occur, sooner or later.

.   .   .

I adhere to the word "victim" rather than "survivor" in the same way that I have chosen to acknowledge what happened to me as "rape" rather than "sexual assault." Others characterize their experience differently, for excellent reasons that I would never seek to contradict. For me, "victim" comes closest to the heart of the matter. I cannot claim agency in this entire episode, because I didn't have any. Whether I survived or not was something that lay wholly in my rapist's hands. In the end I lived because he decided to let me live. And I'm still unable completely to shake off the thought that if anything I did contributed to that outcome, it might have been purchased at too high a price.

There is a distinction to be drawn between recognizing one's own victimization and wallowing in victimhood. I agree with the man who said that the most dangerous emotion in the world is not hatred but self-pity. Not because it turns one into an intolerable puddle of gloom, burdensome to one's friends and relatives and offensive to the neighbors, but because under the influence of self-pity, there is nothing of which one is not capable. As became clear to me that night, and clearer still in its aftermath, my rapist felt sorrier for himself than anybody I have ever met. Whatever richly merited suffering I might experience, he believed, was as dust in the balance in comparison with the wrongs that I and others had done to him, a trivial recompense for the endless sacrifices he had made throughout his priestly ministry. In his eyes he was not committing rape, but doing justice. Both he and I were getting what we truly deserved.

I have little patience with those who offer their victim status as an excuse for bad conduct. Having been sexually abused exempts no one from the obligation of behaving like a human being, the first and most inflexible requirement of which is not to harm others. My instinct to believe those who disclose prior abuse inverts itself in the case of sex offenders, who unlike the rest of us derive benefit rather than harm from advancing these claims. But even if their histories of ill treatment are proven, they may enjoy my sympathy as readily from behind bars, while they serve their sentences, as from anywhere else.

Victimization, though, is a reality, and too often a very grim one. I wish nothing but the best to those who are following a therapeutic path, and who find hope and healing in it. I would like to see many more resources and options available for them than the criminally inadequate levels of provision in countries that could well afford to do far more than they are currently doing.

Still, not everyone can be reached by these means. For some of the most damaged and vulnerable victims of rape, men and women alike, "healing" or "renormalization" may not be possible, and arguably not appropriate even as a theoretical goal. However well intentioned, placing pressure on them to "tell their stories," "reclaim their agency," and transform themselves from "victims" to "survivors" can function simply as another demand to "get with the program" and conform themselves to established psychotherapeutic categories or bureaucratic imperatives—or, in plain English, to make everyone around them feel better by agreeing that they are no longer in pain. When they are unable to do so, the conclusion logically follows that they have no one but themselves to blame if they won't take on the burden of doing the necessary "healing work."

These are assumptions that can kill and, I fear, not infrequently do so. Rape is not just an ordeal to be endured; for some it is a death sentence with an indeterminate stay of execution. Many victims do benefit from the standard therapeutic model. But others are unable to meet the demands it makes of them, or to cope with the (implicit or explicit) victim-blaming that ensues from their inability to comply with its requirements. For them, the challenge is not "healing"—an impossibly remote or unrealistic goal—but making it through the next twenty-four hours without killing themselves. If they are handled clumsily and insensitively, even that limited objective might appear unachievable.

Once again, the metaphors we use matter. Rape victims are not "broken" individuals who need fixing, or sick persons who need healing. They are hurt women and men who need compassion in the face of grievous misfortune. Some of them won't ever get over it, no matter how hard they try. I don't know what compelling reason exists to make them feel that they have to.

6

On Unsatisfactory Resolutions

ONE WINTER'S DAY IN THE MID-1990S I FOUND A MESSAGE at my workplace saying that the police in my home country wanted to get in contact with me. I called the number they had left and found myself speaking with a male detective in the sex crimes unit. It turned out that in the face of mounting public pressure, the Church had finally begun to hand over the files it held on cases of clerical sexual offenses to the civil authorities. One of them was mine.

Many things had changed since I had made my original complaint. I was no longer a teenager, but had finished my doctorate and was holding a position with a high-profile employer that at least *sounded* impressive, for all that my paycheck gave conclusive evidence to the contrary. While none of that should have been relevant to my credibility as a witness, the fact remained that my word would carry more weight now than it had then. The lid had blown off the Church's gruesome recent history of sexual abuse and stories such as mine were no longer reflexively being dismissed as attention-seeking fantasies. The law had changed, with the criminal ban on homosexual acts no longer applying—thereby eliminating the theoretical possibility that an unsuccessful complaint might expose me to prosecution. The crime that had been committed against me was now unambiguously defined as rape, with a maximum potential penalty of life imprisonment.

The officer to whom I spoke was helpful and considerate. He told me that, as I had always feared might be the case, there was evidence to indicate that my rapist had continued to victimize other young men and boys. The sex crimes unit was actively pursuing several lines of inquiry. Would I be willing, he asked, to return home and give evidence in court in the event of a prosecution being brought forward? I told him that I would do so without hesitation if the authorities considered it helpful, although I had little interest in pursuing the rapist purely on my own account.

The mills of justice ground exceedingly slowly. It wasn't until four years later that the police finally felt confident enough to question the priest; seven before he was formally charged; and ten before he was convicted. In the end it was decided not to prosecute him for my rape, but for several others against a much younger boy that he had perpetrated eighteen months afterward. My testimony would not be required after all. Reading between the lines of the various trial reports, it seems that many other outstanding complaints against him were dropped in exchange for a guilty plea. He received a lengthy prison sentence. In light of his parlous health, though—the result of his having burned out his liver as a consequence of lifelong alcohol abuse—the sentence was suspended. To this day, he has not served any time at all in jail for his crimes.

A few years ago, an official state inquiry was conducted to examine how my rapist, and so many like him, had gotten away with their crimes for so long. The report that resulted was lengthy, detailed, and damning. It was revealed not only that the Church had deliberately skirted the criminal law, becoming an accessory after the fact to numerous cases of rape and sexual assault by concealing information or transferring offenders out of the country, but that in many instances these actions had been abetted by the police, who seemed to consider their highest duty to be not to enforce the sex-crimes laws but to assist the Church hierarchy in avoiding a public scandal.

The chapter on my own case made fascinating reading. I learned that several years before I was attacked, my future rapist's clerical superiors arranged for him to undergo a psychiatric evaluation. I don't know who the doctors were who examined him, but if I ever find out, I want to hand out their business cards and recommend them to all my friends. The priest, they told his bosses, should not be placed in a parish setting. In addition to confusion over his sexual identity, he had a deep personality disorder that they did not hesitate to characterize as psychopathic. He would need constant oversight throughout his clerical career. Despite this alarmingly specific report, his bishop returned him to unsupervised parochial duty eight months later. Some years after that, I was to learn the uncanny accuracy of my rapist's clinical evaluation at first hand.

Another interesting element of the report was the information it provided on both the priest's current mentality and that of his superiors. Not only did he adamantly deny ever having assaulted or harmed anyone, but when he was questioned by the police, both he and his powerful supporters in the diocesan bureaucracy expressed outrage that he was being forced to divert attention from the overriding priority of attending to his own physical and mental health to answer the allegations being made against him. A document in the file castigated his accusers, myself presumably included, for our lack of Christian consideration for him. No doubt this is why, months after the police appeared on the scene, the Church was still trying to find yet another pastoral assignment for him.

Lastly, it emerged that the nature of the Church's initial response to my reporting of the attack was not, as I had for many years supposed, the result of individual failings on the part of the clerics concerned, but rather the application of standard operating procedures. The Capuchin priest who conferred absolution upon me unasked and who sedulously avoided learning the identity of my rapist was applying techniques that had been taught to seminarians decades earlier—and that had been used to stifle the complaints of other victims who disclosed their abuse to church authorities. Trainee priests were told by their professors never to seek the names of colleagues against whom complaints about sexual offenses had been made, on the ground that if they were to do so, they might incur an obligation to do something with the knowledge. It wasn't clear from the report what additional justification was advanced to the clerical students for treating the reporting of a criminal offense as a matter requiring the thrusting of absolution and the imposition of penance upon the person making the report. But that practice hardly requires explanation. If one wishes to shield a criminal and cover up his crimes, authoritatively assuring the victim that in the eyes of God he or she is also guilty of sinful conduct and deserving of punishment makes it far more likely that the secret will be kept.

The final outcome of the trial process could, I suppose, be considered a partial vindication, a few of my rapist's chickens coming home to roost. If justice has not been done, some of the truth, at least, is now known. In light of the devastation he caused to others, though, I can take little satisfaction in that. I was not his first victim. But I might have been his last. Rather than facilitating that outcome, the Church not only concealed the crime but abetted it, sending him out of the country where he would be beyond the reach of the law. It did so both to protect its pristine image and, no doubt, because it thought itself bound, in light of the worldwide shortage of priests, to continue making use of even the most flawed human material. To that end it placed what its actions indicate that it recognized as a wolf in a clerical collar back in the midst of an unsuspecting flock, with results that were not so much predictable as inevitable.

Learning the other side of the story (or as much of it as I was able to gather from a report written in judicialese and making the maximum possible use of the passive voice) caused me to look again at my attitudes toward both my rapist and the Church of which we are both a part. In the immediate aftermath of the attack, I had wondered about his motivations. Specifically, I wanted to know "Why me?" Objectively, there was no reason for him to have made me the focus of his attentions. I had been in his company on perhaps half a dozen occasions, always with several others of the same age present. I called him "Father"; he called me by my first name—an uninvited liberty that symbolized the power differential between us. At the time of the attack the expression "batshit crazy" had not yet entered the lexicon, but if it had, his fantasizing into existence some kind of long-standing personal relationship between us would have made it perfectly applicable. His delusion in this respect was what I found most frightening of all, more even than the hysteria or the violence he displayed. Somebody who had lost touch with reality to such a degree was capable of anything.

Had this all been a trap laid for me specifically? There was a good deal of evidence to that effect. The priest would have had to get my telephone number from one of my friends: we weren't in the directory. He would have needed to know which evening of the seven was my night off. Then there were the signs of premeditation in the way the attack had been carried out. He had exaggerated his state of drunkenness to get me to help him into bed (I wished in retrospect that we had not spent so much time watering his drinks). The manner in which he induced me to lie down beside him in a way that minimized my chances of escape or resistance was calculated, cunning—and practiced. This can't have been the first time he'd worked that trick.

But some facts told in the other direction. I might have declined his invitation, and indeed I nearly did, not being keen on a journey by motorbike to the parochial house on a cold, rainy night. Nor could he possibly have known that I would be the last man standing at the party. Somebody else might have drawn the short straw in my place, or we might have decided that his alcoholic condition was not our problem and all departed together. Admittedly, none of this is inconsistent with a preplanned attack against me taking place at some other time, if he hadn't managed to get me where he wanted me on that particular night.

Rightly or wrongly, in light of the number of crimes for which he was responsible over the years, I've concluded that whichever of us turned out to be alone with him that night was probably going to end up getting raped. I freely admit that this may be nothing more than wishful thinking on my part. It enables me to salvage something from the wreckage by letting me believe that I wound up taking a bullet, so to speak, that would otherwise have struck one of my friends. It also means that, if true, I don't have to confront the more disturbing possibility of my having been stalked for an indeterminate period of time without being aware of it.

In the end, though, it doesn't really matter. Rapists rape, and perhaps even they don't know why. Of greater significance was how I was going to respond. The edicts of my faith seemed clear, and all too uncompromising. I had no right to bear malice. *Love your enemies; do good to those who hate you; bless those who curse you; pray for those who abuse you.* And again: *If your brother sins, rebuke him; and if he repents, forgive him.*

Those were hard sayings, and the more I dwelled upon them, the angrier I became. Once again, unilateral obligations were being loaded—even by the Almighty, it seemed—onto the victims of rape, none onto the perpetrators. It was all of a piece with the actions of the Capuchin friar whose response had been to preoccupy himself entirely with the sins I had committed, not to demand that my rapist atone for his. (I never got around to doing the penance prescribed for me that afternoon, nor, I think, will I ever do so. There is a limit.)

Still, if I could not offer my rapist a free pardon, I was surprised to find how sharply I recoiled from the idea of revenge. From the very beginning I felt a strong conviction that the hand that brought him to justice, if that should ever happen, ought not to be mine. Part of it stemmed from the same impulse as my response to demands that I forgive my assailant. Here was yet another unwanted duty that I was supposed to discharge, another example of the privatization of the harm of rape. Other crimes affecting a person's bodily integrity are properly treated as offenses against the community as well as the victim, for which the community has both the right and duty to seek retribution. To murder or to assault someone with impunity is to diminish respect for the human dignity of all, a social value that the collective has a vital interest in defending. Only in the case of rape, and more especially the rape of men, does it seem that the general inclination is to abdicate this responsibility to the victim. His dignity alone is at stake; to him alone falls the task of restoring it, by an equally spectacular display of cathartic counterviolence.

Everything within me rejected, and continues to reject, this outrageously self-serving formula that lets everybody off the hook except the person who has been raped. Punishing the priest's crimes is not my business; it is something that society owes both to me and to itself. Nor is it proper to demand of me that I demonstrate my entitlement to the esteem of others by obliterating the essential difference between myself and my rapist—his willingness, and my refusal, to brutalize another human being for the purpose of self-gratification.

What then of forgiveness, of the Christian charity in respect of which he and his clerical friends have upbraided me and his other accusers for withholding from him? My thinking on this has evolved over the years, as has the way I read the scriptures that once upset me so much. I no longer regard them as an unconditional commandment to do violence to the truth, or to myself. Nor is forgiveness something that unrepentant perpetrators are owed as of right. Quite the contrary: the debt is owed by the perpetrator to the victim. In most cases, demands that somebody forgive a person who has done him or her great harm—or worse, assertions that "healing" is impossible for the victim until forgiveness is spontaneously offered, an assertion to which Christians are particularly prone—reflect nothing more or less than bystanders' discomfort with the spectacle of a continuing injustice and of the suffering of the person experiencing it. Easier by far to browbeat the victim into agreeing that the injustice no longer exists than to acknowledge the obligation of redress that would otherwise fall upon them. Speaking as a believer, I say that to present him or her with such a demand is itself sinful. Even if pardon were an unmitigated good in every circumstance and all situations, which is far from the case, if worthy of the name it must be absolutely uncoerced, not extorted at the point of a theological or therapeutic bayonet.

Forgiveness, in the true sense, is both functional and relational. It does not deny the existence of the original fault, or minimize the gravity of the damage done; rather it insists on the acknowledgment and redress of both. To be effective, it requires the full and active cooperation of the person to be forgiven, a condition generally known as repentance. Without that essential component, the extending of premature forgiveness is not just futile but positively harmful to the perpetrator him- or herself, an invitation to go on offending rather than doing the necessary work of restitution (to the limited extent that that is possible) and self-rehabilitation.

In my rapist's specific case, the only forgiveness I am able to offer him without his participation is in the original, narrow sense of the word: the voluntary giving-up of the right to collect on a debt owed. For what little it will be worth to him, he has this. As my faith reasonably demands of me, I have renounced any claim of private revenge upon him. I do not want him to experience harm as I was harmed, now or in the future, and not simply (though it is so) because I do not believe I could ever make him suffer as he has made me suffer. But I do not have the power to restore to him the quality of full humanity from which he has voluntarily and disastrously cut himself off by his actions; he alone does. To gain true forgiveness, he needs true repentance. At minimum this would require a public confession on his part of his offenses, against me and all the others he has harmed, and the uncomplaining acceptance by him of the temporal penalties due for those offenses. The debt he owes society is entirely separate and distinct from the debt he owes us. Forgiveness, moreover, is not synonymous with reconciliation. Because full restitution in cases of rape or sexual abuse is impossible—while the victim may, in some cases, recover his or her physical and spiritual wholeness, it does not lie within the perpetrator's ability to make that happen—there can be no question of reverting to the status quo ante. Even if the rapist is a relative, he or she has permanently forfeited any claim to further contact of any kind, except in those rare instances in which it occurs at the victim's initiative and on the victim's terms. Normally that will not happen, and because sexual offenders have already proven their dangerousness, no victim should ever be asked to expose him- or herself to the risk, in the name of forgiveness or anything else.

Every year or so I run the priest's name through a search engine to find out if he has died, and am slightly disappointed to discover that thus far he has not. (Clearly, some work of my own remains for me to do in the forgiveness department.) Still, though I don't really expect that he's likely to do so, I genuinely hope that in the time remaining to him he will take some steps in the direction not so much of seeking forgiveness, but of equipping himself to be able to benefit from it. What little I know of how he has conducted his life thus far serves as confirmation of C. S. Lewis's observation that the gates of Hell are fastened on the inside. In my own personal understanding of the scheme of creation, everyone has the right to be as self-centered, as preoccupied with their own wants, impulses, and desires, as they wish, in this life and in the one to come. But eternity is a very long time indeed to spend with one's focus fixed exclusively upon oneself. All the more so if one wasn't a particularly nice person to begin with.

My attitude toward the Church is more complicated. Before the attack my faith was important to me, and I was a weekly churchgoer. Afterward, things changed. I did not storm off in a display of righteous anger, which actually would have been far more positive and healthy than what I wound up doing. Instead, I simply drifted away, all the while telling myself that my convictions about God and the moral order had not altered in the slightest. For three or four years, church was an Easter and Christmas duty for me, and I isolated myself spiritually as much as I had already done physically. In the end I decided I was behaving irrationally. Still professing membership in a Church I never attended made as much sense as claiming that I was an athlete, just one who never took any exercise. It seemed to me that I needed to make up my mind about whether I still believed in my religion or not, and conduct myself accordingly.

In the end I concluded that I did, and that it was necessary for me to distinguish between the creed and the crime. So exceptionally flawed an individual, I decided, was not to be taken as an authentic representative of two millennia of Christian faith and practice, merely because of the use of a clerical collar that it seems clear he saw as nothing more than a hunting license. From a more bloody-minded standpoint, I was unwilling to allow my rapist to run me out of my Church on top of all the other losses he had inflicted upon me. My decision to remain a Catholic was made without qualification or reservation. I adhere to the faith because, believing it to be true, I consider it my duty to do so. And I should most certainly not wish anything I have written here to stand in the way of anyone at a similar point in his or her faith journey from doing likewise.

But although I have returned to the practice of the faith that gives my life meaning, so far as the instinctive attitude of trust I had previously reposed in the leadership of the Church is concerned, things have never been quite the same. Somehow, if forgiveness were part of the equation, I found it easier to forgive my attacker, who is clearly a moral imbecile lacking the capacity to see others as anything but instruments for his own gratification. The men who had unleashed him upon me, and upon others after me, were in another category entirely. So too were those fellow clerics who knew or had excellent reason to suspect what he, and thousands like him, truly were, but said and did nothing. The "good Germans" who themselves abused nobody but heard the rumors, saw the drinking and the sexual acting out, watched the parade of young people to the parish halls and the rectories, listened to the confessions, and placed their careers or their desires for a quiet life ahead of the welfare of their flocks—theirs is a heavy responsibility, for which one day they will have to answer. So must the regrettably large number of those persons who, through minimization of the crimes, marginalization of the injured, and exercise of a preferential option for the perpetrators, lend themselves to the ongoing process of revictimization. Closure is not to be obtained by contemptuously tossing the contents of the collection basket in the direction of the minority of victims who have been compelled to resort to the civil courts to seek some inadequate portion of what the Hierarchy's collective conscience was insufficient to concede, and thereafter consigning the entire episode to some capacious Orwellian memory hole. The Church has many injustices in this regard to redress, and the work of atonement has hardly yet begun.

.   .   .

While writing this chapter, I take a brief trawl through the news sites for just the past few weeks. In the Afghan city of Herat, a five-year-old boy is raped until his assailants realize that "the life of the child was in danger." He dies on the way to hospital, a victim of what the US State Department describes as a "widespread, culturally sanctioned form of male rape" in that country. In Newcastle in northeast England, a twenty-four-year-old man is subjected to a "horrific ordeal" after accepting a lift home from a stranger. A detective inspector of the local Rape Investigation Team says, "My message to men is they need to think about their own safety as much as women do and try not to put themselves in vulnerable situations." A Nova Scotia mother complains about the leniency of a two-year sentence awarded to one of the three men who kidnapped her son under the pretext of offering him a job, chained him blindfolded to a bed in a remote log cabin, threatened him with death, and raped him repeatedly during an eight-day captivity. At seven-thirty in the morning, a sixty-nine-year-old grandfather is raped while out for his daily run in a public park in Tennessee. In the neighboring state of Alabama, the judiciary, in a revision of its criminal code, decides to begin prosecuting violent sexual attacks upon men and boys as "rape" rather than "sodomy" or "aggravated assault"; overnight, the proportion of such cases as a percentage of all rapes jumps from zero to 13 percent. The Mongolian government, proceeding determinedly in the opposite direction, is criticized for not prosecuting the assailants of a gay man who was sexually tortured, because "male-on-male rape is not covered in the criminal code." An Oxford University researcher reports that of more than four thousand nongovernmental organizations working in the field of war rape and sexual abuse, only 3 percent mention the existence of the sexual victimization of boys and men in their literature—"typically," one of her colleagues notes, "as a passing reference." A journalist from the *Observer* in London describes a massive wave of war rape of men in Central Africa, one aid worker telling him that the wives of these men often leave them in disgust. "They ask me, 'So now how am I going to live with him? As what? Is this still a husband? Is it a wife?'" A doctor with a refugee center in Kampala "has now seen so many male survivors that, frequently, she can spot them the moment they sit down. 'They tend to lean forward and will often sit on one buttock. . . . When they cough, they grab their lower regions. At times, they will stand up and there's blood on the chair.'" According to a professor at the UCLA School of Law, 21 percent of Sri Lankan men seen by a London treatment center had suffered sexual torture while in detention; 80 percent of a sample of six thousand male concentration-camp prisoners in Sarajevo admitted they had been raped.

The list could be extended indefinitely. It would appear that there are a great deal more of us out there than people imagine.

What is to be done? To recycle the cliché, the first step in dealing with the problem is to acknowledge its existence. Men are raped, all over the world and on a daily basis. They are raped in prison and out; in cars and public places; in schools and the armed services; in colleges and at camps; on friends' sofas and in their own homes. Their rapists are colleagues, strangers, pastors, casual acquaintances, relatives, close friends, lovers, and spouses. Nobody knows just how many victims there are, but all the indications are that it's a very large number indeed. In light of the fact that under present circumstances perpetrators are almost guaranteed to get away with it, it would be astonishing if it were otherwise.

If there is a second source of consensus, it is in the fact that social and legal provision for male victims comes in only two varieties: inadequate and nonexistent. There are many reasons for this, but by far the most important is an extremely high level of rape denial, rape apology, and rape minimization—a set of prejudicial attitudes that have recently gone under the umbrella term of "rape culture"—prevalent throughout a wide variety of societies with respect to men who have been raped. Simply put, if men wished to disclose their victimization, there are alarmingly few venues in which it would be safe for them to do so. Such studies as have been carried out are almost unanimous in finding that health-care professionals, law enforcement officers, nongovernmental organizations, and the general public tend "to be skeptical about reports of male sexual assault unless these reports involve male children." As one researcher has recently noted, "The intense stigma of same-sex rape is enough to prevent most male survivors from obtaining the services they need unless physical injuries severely compromise the survivor's life or ability to hide the assault from others."

These findings ring true to me. The impediments they highlight are precisely the same factors that deterred me from reporting my own rape to the police three decades ago and made it impossible for me to obtain any effective assistance afterward. It is difficult for me to find words to express my disappointment that so little has changed even in the most highly developed countries in the intervening years.

There is, though, a relevant history here. Fifty or sixty years ago, in most Western countries, the state of affairs for female rape victims was little better, if at all, than for their male counterparts today. Rape crisis centers did not appear on the scene until the early 1970s; the numbers of reported rapes in Europe and North America were anywhere from a fifth to well under a tenth of the current figures; medical protocols, where they existed at all, often revictimized women and girls seeking treatment; several important categories of offense, like marital rape, did not exist; and the ordeal of reporting sex crimes to the authorities and obtaining a conviction was even more forbidding than it is at present. It was only by dint of a long and tortuous process of voluntary organization, consciousness raising, political lobbying, and scholarly research that the needle was shifted in a more positive direction. It may be that the same will need to be done to obtain adequate services and procedures for male victims, though I would hope that it will not prove necessary to reinvent the wheel in every single instance.

But before that can happen, men who have been raped will have to come out of the shadows. Attitudes are not changed by statistics or abstract appeals to equality, but by being able to match stories to names, and names to faces. When I was raped, I was unable to find a single account more recent than the couple of paragraphs in Lawrence of Arabia's autobiography to tell me what it was like for men, what kinds of feelings I might experience, or what problems I was likely to encounter. For very good reasons, nobody else was willing to put his head above the parapet. Nor, with a very few magnificently reckless exceptions, have others done so since then.

A start has to be made somewhere. This is my attempt at one.

Sources

These notes apply to material on pages 103–107.

"widespread, culturally sanctioned": 2009 *Human Rights Report: Afghanistan*, March 11, 2010, US Department of State, http://www.state.gov/j/drl/rls/hrrpt/2009/sca/136084.htm.

"In Newcastle": Sophie Doughty, "Detectives Urge Men to Think About Their Safety as They Investigate a Male Rape in Newcastle," *Evening Chronicle* (Newcastle, UK), July 2, 2014.

"A Nova Scotia mother": "John Leonard MacKean Gets Two Years for Sexually Assaulting Chained-Up Nova Scotia Teen," *Toronto Star*, June 24, 2014.

"At seven-thirty": Claire Wiseman, "Mother of Teen Accused of Raping Jogger in North Chattanooga Says 'He's a good child,'" *Chattanooga Times Free Press*, October 2, 2014.

"In the neighboring state": Tim Lockette, "New Numbers Correct Undercount of Rapes in Alabama," *Anniston (AL) Star*, July 28, 2014.

"The Mongolian government": Andrew Potts, "Mongolian Government Plans to Protect LGBTIs from Hate Crimes," *Gay Star News*, June 23, 2014.

"An Oxford University researcher": Saipira Furstenberg, "Male Rape in Armed Conflicts: Why We Should Talk About It," *Oxford Human Rights Hub*, July 1, 2014, http://ohrh.law.ox.ac.uk /male-rape-in-armed-conflicts-why-we-should-talk-about-it/; Lara Stemple, "Male Rape and Human Rights," *Hastings Law Journal* 60 (February 2009): 612.

"A doctor with a refugee center": Will Storr, "The Rape of Men," *Observer*, July 17, 2011.

"According to a professor": Stemple, "Male Rape and Human Rights," 613–14.

"the numbers of reported rapes in Europe and North America": Figures based on the following: (United States) US Department of Justice, Federal Bureau of Investigation, *Crime in the United States: Uniform Crime Reports—1961* (Washington, DC: Government Printing Office, 1961), 2; US Department of Justice, Federal Bureau of Investigation, *Crime in the United States 2012: Uniform Crime Reports*, http://www.fbi.gov/about-us /cjis/ucr/crime-in-the-u.s/2012/crime-in-the-u.s.-2012/violent -crime/rape; (Great Britain) Parliamentary Debates, House of Commons, 661 *H.C. Deb.* 5s., c. 82W (June 7, 1962); R. A. Carr-Hill and N. H. Stern, *The Police and Criminal Statistics: An Analysis of Official Statistics for England and Wales using Econometric Methods* (London: Academic Press, 1979), 119, table 4.A.1.; Office of National Statistics, *Focus on: Violent Crime and Sexual Offences 2011/12*, table 1.02, http://ons.gov .uk/ons/rel/crime-stats/crime-statistics/focus-on-violent-crime/rft -appendix-tables.xls; (Scotland) Scottish Home Department, *Criminal Statistics Scotland 1960: Statistics Relating to Police Apprehensions and Criminal Proceedings for the year 1960*, Cmnd. 1343 (Edinburgh, HMSO, 1961), 29, table 4; Scottish Government, *Recorded Crime in Scotland 2012–13*, p. 31, table A2, and p. 39, table A3, http://www.gov.scot/Resource /0042/00427834.pdf; (France) V. Veeraraghavan, *Rape and Victims of Rape* (New Delhi: Northern Book Centre, 1987), 3;

Observatoire national de la délinquance et de réponses pénales, "Criminalité et délinquance enregistrées en 2009: Les faits constatés par les services de police et les unités de gendarmerie," *Bulletin pour l'année 2009*, January 2010, 9, http://www .memoiretraumatique.org/assets/files/Documents-pdf/Bulletin _annuel_2009_Observatoire-national-de-la-delinquance_ONDRP .pdf; (Germany) G. Schulz, *Die Notzucht: Täter-Opfer -Situationen* (Hamburg: Verlag für kriminalistische Fachliteratur, 1958), 32, table 2; Bundesministerium des Innen, *Polizeiliche Kriminalstatistik 2011* (Berlin: BdI, 2012), 45, table 5.